Puppet on a String

After working as a research assistant in the psychiatric department of a Zulu hospital, Helena Wilkinson trained in counselling. For four years she was the Editor of *Carer and Counsellor*. She is the author of six books and numerous booklets, and is a member of the Society of Authors and the Society of Women Writers and Journalists. Helena was the Founder of Kainos Trust for eating disorders, and operated as Director until January 2004 when she joined the full-time team of Nicholaston House, a Christian healing centre on Gower, attached to Swansea City Mission.

Unless otherwise stated all biblical quotations are taken from the Good News Bible, which was the Bible the author read at the time of writing the first edition of *Puppet on a String*.

Other books by Helena Wilkinson published by RoperPenberthy Publishing Ltd are:

Beyond Chaotic Eating
Breaking Free From Loneliness

Dedicated to everyone with anorexia,
as a message of hope.

PUPPET ON A STRING

HELENA WILKINSON

RoperPenberthy Publishing Ltd
Horsham, England

Published by RoperPenberthy Publishing Ltd
PO Box 545, Horsham, England RH12 4QW

First published in Great Britain in 1984
by Hodder & Stoughton Ltd
Updated version published by
RoperPenberthy Publishing Ltd 2004

ISBN 1 903905 18 4

Cover design by Angie Moyler

Typeset by Avocet Typeset, Chilton, Aylesbury, Bucks
Printed in the United Kingdom by Cox & Wyman Ltd,
Reading, Berkshire

CONTENTS

PUPPET ON A STRING

From everyone around
There's hardly a sound,
As she fades away
Day after day,
Until painfully thin,
No more than bones and skin.

Life vanishing fast,
She's fled her cast
And stands in solitude
Letting no one intrude.
In a world of her own
No happiness is sown.

Pitiful and dejected
Is the image she's reflected,
Tearful and drooping,
She's a puppet on a string
And her last thread
Is between the living and the dead.

(Aged 17)

TWENTY YEARS ON

Twenty years have passed since I wrote *Puppet on a String* and one of the main questions you may be asking is, 'Have you ever gone back into anorexia?' The most commonly held beliefs are that once someone has been anorexic there is a vulnerability to it, so under stress the person is likely to retreat into the same patterns or can never be free from the desire to control their eating. The answer to the question of whether I have ever gone back into anorexia is, 'No, I haven't.' I do not live in fear of ever going back, nor do I live a life one step away from it, still controlled by thoughts about food and weight. I now live a life *totally* free from anorexia and I know that I would *never* go back under any circumstances.

How can I be so sure that I will not even be tempted to carry out anorexic patterns? Anorexia serves a purpose for people: it is their way of coping with life when they do not know how else to cope; it is their means of being in control in what feels like a frightening world because they cannot communicate, do not know how to set boundaries or lack confidence; and it is their form of identity when there appear to be unanswerable questions about their value as a person.

The reason I can be sure that I will not even be tempted to carry out anorexic patterns is because it no longer serves a purpose for me! At the time I suffered from anorexia it had been my way of coping with being partially sighted; with the terrible emotional and physical bullying I endured at school; with sexual abuse; with self-hatred and lack of confidence. I was fearful of the adult world and unable to communicate: I needed anorexia to take my focus away from these things. At 18, when I became a Christian, I made a conscious decision not to cope with life's hurdles through anorexia. In addition I began a process of being helped to strengthen the areas which had been weaknesses and could have led to relapse: communication; boundaries; confidence; worth; etc., and moved forward, not only leaving the anorexia behind but knowing that I would never return to it. I moved from being *simply recovered* to being *totally free* from anorexia, although I knew that emotional healing and recovery from the effects of the past might take much longer.

When I started writing *Puppet on a String* I did so as a means of getting things out of my system, and not for publication. I did not think for one minute that anyone would want to read what I had written – I had never spoken with another anorexic, never read a book on the subject, and as far as writing was concerned I had failed my English Language O level twice, only a year or two earlier! Yet I had a strong conviction that people needed to know how anorexics *feel* on the inside. When I submitted *Puppet on a String* for publication as a hesitant and shy 19 year-old I half expected the literary agent to laugh; instead he wrote, 'I'm delighted to take on your book. It really does merit publication. You write well, the content is compulsive, and many will be helped by it.' Although he said that the acceptance rate with the publisher he had chosen was only three manuscripts in every thousand submitted, as soon as I received his letter I knew that the book would be published, my message heard, and I had a feeling that this was only the beginning: that there was more to come than simply my book being published.

Little did I realise what 'only the beginning' actually meant! The book became a best-seller and I was inundated with desperate cries for help from anorexics, young and not so young. For eighteen months I gave up my work as a crèche assistant to meet the people who had written to me. As I came face-to-face with them, encountered their pain and shared with them how God had set me free, I not only saw lives restored but learned far more about the people who suffer from eating disorders than any textbook could ever teach me. I knew that I was being called to work with such people.

Still shy, and half wanting to run from the calling, I fled to Zululand in Southern Africa, having been told that anorexia was an unknown phenomenon amongst the rural Zulu people. Within a matter of months the doctor I was working for stumbled across his first case of anorexia in the 26 years he had been working among the rural people. I instantly knew that if you run from your calling the calling comes after you!

After returning to England, for many years I maintained an interest in eating disorders: counselling, speaking and writing on the subject. But it was only a small aspect of my life, and I was certain that one day it would play a more significant role. I still had a lot of learning and changing to do myself, and I entered a period that I can only describe as 'the university of life' where I was faced with trials, hurts and realities about my shortcomings. This turbulent period could have so easily been a vulnerable time for anorexia to take a hold again. The fact that it did not was proof enough that it never would be a part of my life. After training in counselling and then working as the editor of a journal for counsellors for four years my 'university' period reached a climax, with three major losses within one month. This gave birth to something new, when I sensed God say so clearly that now was the time to become fully involved in eating disorders.

I realised then that I was not merely going to work *with* eating disorder sufferers, but was being called to pioneer a unique organisation. When I thought about what to call the organisation one word kept coming to my mind: *Kainos*, a New Testament Greek word meaning 'new but qualitatively different.' It was a new but qualitatively different life that I had found through God setting me free from anorexia, and that I would be involved in leading others towards, and so I set up a charity called Kainos Trust.

I prayed that I would know on what basis to establish Kainos Trust, and as I did so God told me to read the book of Nehemiah in the Old Testament, saying that there were parallels between Nehemiah's vision and work and mine. Someone brought to Nehemiah's attention the broken walls of the city of Jerusalem: as he stood amidst the crumbled city he wept, not just for the physical ruins he saw, but for where the city was spiritually. What lay before Nehemiah, to the eyes of many, looked hopeless. Yet he could see *beyond* the ruins to a potentially beautiful city. He prayed and followed whatever God said he must do to rebuild that city. People mocked his ideas for restoration, but he knew that because *God* had a strategy it would work. And it did!

The crumbled city walls are like all the broken areas of the lives of those with eating disorders. People look at the 'mess' and declare that it can never be *fully* restored. But, like Nehemiah, God has given me the ability to see behind the obvious to what can be. When I look at a person with an eating disorder I do not see the hopelessness of an addictive pattern which seems impossible to break, but the freedom which could be: the potential for a new and qualitatively different life, when someone puts into operation the necessary physical, emotional and spiritual principles for freedom. Kainos Trust was established to show that *full* recovery, *freedom* is possible, and to give guidelines as to how to take such steps.

Within one month of operating and without advertising we had 400 members! People made contact from far and wide and from all spheres of life. Eating disorders cut across age, sex and race. Over the years I have worked with young children, older people, male and female, and I have been asked to speak not only in affluent countries but even third world countries, such as Zimbabwe, where there are pockets of Westernised lifestyle and thinking which lead to Westernised ways of coping. Wherever I am asked to speak and for however long, whether a short talk or comprehensive teaching over several days, there is one point I *never* fail to make – people with eating disorders can *fully* recover and no longer be vulnerable to relapse. I hope that twenty years of full recovery and some very painful situations on route have proved that it is possible not to retreat back into anorexia.

Eating disorders remain a significant part of my life, and I will always have compassion for those held in its grip, but more recently God has opened up my work far beyond eating disorders. In January 2004 Kainos Trust began working alongside Swansea City Mission and I became a part of the full-time team at Nicholaston House, which comes under the Mission. The House has a heart for hurting people, some of whom have eating disorders, but many of whom are wrestling with other issues or simply need time out. The balance is good. It reminds me that eating disorders have similar roots to other coping mechanisms, and it is encouraging to see people with different life circumstances, past histories and ways of coping, being impacted, changed and healed.

I end with those incredibly powerful words of Jesus in John's Gospel: 'If you hold to my teaching, you are really my disciples. Then you will know the truth, and the truth will set you free' (John 8:31-32, NIV). My prayer is that in reading, or re-reading, *Puppet on a String*, if you have an eating disorder you will come to know and experience freedom, and if you care for someone with an eating disorder you will be assured that freedom is possible for the one for whom you care. And if you are struggling with any other type of addiction or coping mechanism, you too will come to know freedom and wholeness.

Helena Wilkinson
Nicholaston House,
Penmaen, Gower, Swansea 2004

1 | LOOKING AND SEEING

When I look
What do I see?

But a primrose so sweet
And so neat,

A daisy white as snow,
Grass that will ever grow,

The birds that fly overhead
To their nesty bed,

The clouds that glide along
As a bird will sing its song,

The sweet clover
That everyone treads over,

The roaring sea
That splashes me.

That's what I see.

(Aged 10)

I made a very hurried entry into the world. The gynaecologist who was supposed to be present at my birth had not even reached the labour room in time to see me arrive!

The midwife seized me and desperately tried to unravel the umbilical cord that was tied several times around my neck and twisted in and out. Anxiously she endeavoured to prevent it from strangling me. Her face hot and bothered and her glasses steamed up, she managed it. I had arrived alive and kicking!

All the routine procedures of cleaning me up, making sure I was breathing properly and checking my weight took place. I was a mere 5 pounds 7 ounces, and had received virtually no nutrition during my last days in the womb since the umbilical cord had been so tightly twisted around my neck. The doctors said that if I had arrived a week later (when I was due) I would have been dead. Had I been born in England there might have been more concern over my physical state, but since I was born in Africa the most important factor was that I was alive!

There was no early contact with my mother. I was shown to her, then placed in a cot at the end of a separate ward. Babies in Africa, at that time, were made to sleep through the night and were not fed, regardless of their weight.

Whilst in hospital for that first week, the only period during the day at which my mother could make contact with me was feeding time. There was no chance for mother and child to develop a warm relationship, for the mother to cuddle her newly-born baby. Even during the short time I was feeding there was continuous noise and cigarette smoke from the visitors – visiting and feeding coincided and so feeding was a very tense time.

At the end of our time in the Princess Elizabeth Hospital in Nairobi, the capital of Kenya, my father came to pick us up. With him were my elder sister, Ruth, who was nearly three, and our Goan nanny, Agnes. They were delighted with the new addition to the family and their excitement mounted as the car wound its way up the long steep hill and down again through the shady eucalyptus trees to Muguga, where we lived.

My father was a forest entomologist and we lived on the edge of a research station, in an attractive bungalow which looked out over the forest to the distant blue ridge of the Ngong Hills. The garden was a landscape of its own. Its valley, outdoor theatre and fascinating collection of magnificent rocks and cacti contrasted with the cascades of riotous colour of the bougainvillaea on the house and the sweet fragrance of the lily garden.

At the back of our bungalow was a lovely nursery, which Ruth and I were to share. She had a bed by one window surrounded by all her zoo animals, whilst my Moses basket was placed in the cot at the other end.

Ruth was happy to have 'her baby' in the nursery with her, but the novelty soon wore off when I cried throughout each night. I screamed so much that I ended up sleeping in the pram in my parents' room so that I could be rocked and wheeled around. My mother tried cuddling me, night after night, but still I cried. Nothing would comfort me for long. Eventually the doctor came out from Nairobi, and after pacing up and down the room quite obviously debating what to do, he said that he would like me to be admitted to hospital.

I was taken to the children's hospital and sedated with Chloral. My mother came in every day to feed me, and after about a week I had improved and was allowed home again. It was only a matter of days after leaving hospital that the screaming began again, accompanied by a badly upset stomach which once again affected my sleeping patterns. I was taken back into the children's hospital. On return home, the same thing happened again and I was readmitted. By this time I was on Lactogen baby food made with water, and my mother queried whether the complaint had anything to do with the borehole water which we used in Muguga. This was found to be so. Some of the minerals contained in the water affected me adversely.

Apart from the very disturbed sleeping patterns at night and the tendency to be very startled and frightened if woken during the day, I appeared to be a perfectly normal happy and very sociable baby, lapping up the stimulation of other people. Feeding was not a problem and I happily drank and drank, quite obviously physically yearning for more in order to catch up in weight.

As I developed, although I was very responsive to sound my mother was convinced that I could not see her. She had commented about this earlier when I appeared to be very sensitive to bright light. Everyone else denied the fact, suggesting that it was probably just late development in focusing. The early stages of noticing objects, and in particular the expressions on people's faces, such as a smile portraying happiness or acceptance are very important in early life. A baby's conversation is partially through its response to facial expression. Therefore, a baby without sight is likely to feel frustrated, scared and lonely. These must have been my feelings at such an early and vulnerable stage in life.

Being so convinced that there was something wrong, my mother took me to King George VI Hospital, where Dr Beryl Lake (who later became my godmother) discovered that I had a severe nystagmus and was unable to focus: effectively I was blind – my world consisted not of total darkness, but brilliant light without the ability to focus. An appointment was made to see the eye specialist in the same hospital, who confirmed the diagnosis and wanted some investigations of the optic nerve carried out under anaesthetic. He suggested that since we were considering moving to England this should be done by a Harley Street specialist.

Despite the pain my parents faced knowing that I was unable to see, life carried on as normal. On Palm Sunday, March 22 1964, I was baptised from the director's rose-bowl in a little church on the research station at Muguga. It was a great excitement for everyone present as it was the first baptism in a new church which my parents had helped to build.

On Good Friday we moved into one of the cottages in Muguga House (the main house on the research station) so that my father could pack up the contents of our bungalow in preparation for our move to England. Just under two weeks later we caught the night train to Mombasa, arriving at the Two Fishes Hotel, Diani Beach, run by two lovely people, Beth and Allan Fish. Beth and Allan had no children of their own, but had created a hotel which was a paradise for children, among shady casuarina and palm trees at the edge of the tropical blue sea with its multi-coloured fish and white surf. Ruth loved the expanse of beach with its white sandcastles and the fun of the leaping waves; I was content to kick on the soft, warm sand in the shade of the casuarina trees. Beth and I seemed to have an immediate bond of love, and here with the rhythmic sound of surf in my ears I slept through the night for the first time in my life.

In April 1964 we moved to England; Ruth was aged three-and-a-half and I was seven months. The white sandy beaches, palm trees and crystal-clear water with the mysterious East African sunsets over the hills faded into the distance, no longer a reality but a fairytale memory. After a long delay at the airport and travelling four thousand miles, the plane landed in England at midnight. We took delivery of our new car and drove through the darkness of the night a further hundred miles to Suffolk to stay with my mother's parents, arriving at a very unsociable hour in the morning.

For the following eight months we did not have a base of our own and for the majority of the time lived with Ruth's and my godparents, staying sometimes with relatives, and taking a holiday in a little picturesque cottage in Southwold on the Suffolk coast.

Not long after we had moved to England I was taken to Moorfields Hospital in London to see the eye specialist. I was given the pre-med and left in my carrycot with my father, whilst my mother had to go downstairs to have her eyes checked. When she came back I was screaming and obviously very frightened; immediately she picked me up and walked up and down until I fell asleep, but no sooner was I asleep in her arms than I was woken up for the anaesthetic! From that day on it took two hours of gentle soothing to get me to sleep. I was forcing myself to keep my eyes open, too frightened to sleep.

A month later I went back to Moorfields Hospital for three days of investigations. My mother mentioned to the nursing sister that ever since the last anaesthetic I had fought sleep. Her reply was, 'That sometimes happens with anaesthetics, especially with babies; it could be worse after this time'. It was – I woke every hour of the night for most of the hour, so much so that my mother had to take me into her room as she no longer had the energy to keep walking along the corridor.

My early experiences in life no doubt laid a foundation for insecurity later on. Rudolph Schaffer in his book *Mothering* points out that hospitalisation does have an effect on the child that it is apt to feel later on. He writes:

When we turn to the immediate effects of a child's separation from his mother the picture is much clearer. A young child is likely to experience severance of the bond with his mother as devastating, if, that is, the separation occurs under traumatic circumstances and the child is sent to a strange environment and is there looked after by strangers, as happens, for instance, in hospitalisation or admission to public care.

As it is stipulated that separation before the age of seven months is of little consequence and most of my hospitalisation was before this age, I thought that it could bear no relation to what happened to me later. However, my concept changed when Rudolph Schaffer went on to say:

In the past, separation studies have exclusively concentrated on relatively gross indications such as crying, changes in activity, and sleeping or eating disorders. But in view of the fine synchronisation established between mother and baby from the early weeks on, we ought to consider the possibility that at a much more microscopic level interaction processes can also be disrupted before seven months. Even if the infant reveals no awareness of the mother's absence and therefore shows no separation upset, might not established synchronisation patterns be distorted when someone else takes the mother's place – someone who has not learned the specific characteristics of that particular infant, who may not have the motivation to be as sensitive to his signals as his mother, and whose own behaviour in interaction may be entirely different? If this were the case, some sort of effect would register in the infant's behaviour, though the indications might well be far more subtle than those in separated infants beyond the seven months' milestone.

Looking back I can see that both the separation from my mother and the struggles of having an eyesight problem did have a big effect upon me. But it was not only the early months of my life which were affected and which led to a profound lack of confidence and deep insecurity. The outcome of the eye investigation was that I would gain some sight but that my sight would always be impaired, and living with the reality of this, along with the unhelpful way in which people handled me as a result of my eyesight was very damaging. (Today I am still registered partially sighted, but there is a huge difference in how I now cope with it.)

By Christmas my father had been offered a job with ICI and we moved into a house in Berkshire, situated in a quiet cul-de-sac within walking distance of Wokingham town centre. The house, a chalet bungalow, was new, and the garden, like our Kenyan one, needed to be made, so once again my parents set about creating a home and garden of beauty for us.

I was a bundle of energy; climbing, running and playing. At the age of two I was sent to play school, which

I absolutely adored. There were no problems over being separated from my parents or in being visually impaired: no sooner had I arrived than I was on the swings or splashing around with the paint. I enjoyed every minute of my time there. Then I began to get very bad earache. I remember many a night sleeping with my ear pressed to a hot-water bottle covered with a jumper or a vest. The doctor decided when I was three that my tonsils ought to be removed. Once more the anaesthetic upset me. Apparently I was like a wild tiger when I was trying to fight the dizzy feeling!

I began school at the age of four, at a local infant school. Although very shy, I did not take long to settle and started to enjoy myself almost immediately. My memories are mostly of the art and craft lessons and the big gymnasium full of exciting equipment. Later that year, when I was five I taught myself to roller-skate. I would spend hours speeding up and down the path, making up dances and generally amusing myself.

Just before I was due to start junior school we went on holiday to Ibiza. Here the days were full of fun, exploration and games amongst the whitewashed buildings and the oleander bushes of the hotel courtyard. There were climbing frames and crazy golf, table-tennis and swimming pools, but the greatest joy of all was the freedom of the warm blue sea and being able to swim totally on my own for the first time. Not even a toe on the bottom!

At home again, another new adventure awaited me: starting a new school. My junior school was only a short walk away from our house and brought a mixture of fear and fun, joy and sorrow. The lessons were a challenge which I mostly enjoyed, but with the bigger boys and their rough playground games I was less confident than I had been at infant school. My teachers said I was a silent, shy mouse in contrast to my lively, bouncing ways at home. However, for the most part junior school jogged along quite happily until one terrible, fatal day.

There was a little boy at school of whom I was very fond. We would sit next to each other in class and always be partners; he was the only boy that I really liked. I arrived at school that day to be told by the teacher that he was dead. My heart sank, the classroom felt so empty – a horrible uncanny feeling. I went home and told my mother. There it was in the paper. A father had committed suicide, killing two of his own children at the same time: one of them was my friend Nicholas.

One theory is that anorexia stems from a childhood trauma, a hurt deep down inside. If such a theory were proved I am sure this event would have some significance. To discover death is a frightening and painful enough experience as it is, but when it is linked in with suicide and murder, it becomes quite a different matter.

It was around this time that I began to have bad nightmares and fear the dark, as a lot of children do. Some of the nightmares were so vivid that I still remember the smallest detail, like the colour of the carpet or the faces of the people in the dream. One dream in particular occurred several times over a period of a year or two. I would be lying in bed, my father sitting beside me reading a story. He would switch on the lamp next to my bed and turn out the light by the door. When the story was over he would say goodnight and switch my lamp off. Suddenly the lamp would flash a ray of dazzling colours and a man would step out of the wardrobe. He wore a black coat and his eyes were dark and piercing.

'If I succeed I'll take you away; if I don't I'll be back another day'.

His voice was harsh and sly. He would place his hands on my stomach and press and press and press. With anger and hatred he would say, 'I'll come back again and I'll get you next time'. Then he would disappear back into the wardrobe.

I would wake up with an excruciating pain in my stomach, and very scared. It is rather ironic that such a terrifying dream – a repetitive dream – should be connected with the stomach!

My dreams nearly always expressed fear of the dark, being murdered or desperately trying to escape from something or someone. Another common dream that I had around this time was being in the house, either alone or with the rest of my family, when a burglar broke in. I would always be the one to hear or notice him and would creep downstairs to go and get help from the neighbours. As soon as I had left the drive, he would be following me; my legs would seize up and however much energy I put into the running, my progress would be minuscule – I was trapped. I always woke up just before being caught. The dream would recur with very similar situations, with the house catching fire or a murderer appearing in the house.

In complete contrast, I also dreamt that I had abilities no one else possessed, such as being able to fly. It was not just a magical child's dream where I had instant wings and took off. I would nearly always be playing with my friends when suddenly an odd sensation would come over me – I would then bend my knees and put my hands on my hips, pushing my elbows out. A strange energy-force would enter my body, and I would keep pushing my elbows outwards. It took a lot of concentration and effort but gradually I would feel my feet leave the ground and I would rise higher. The odd thing was that I had to keep in the cramped position in order to keep off the ground. I showed my friends what they had to do but they never seemed to manage it. I could not understand why they seemed so incapable of such an easy task!

I did not know anything about the psychology of dreams other than that dreams are supposed to reveal the subconscious feelings of a person. That was certainly proved when I was developing anorexia, as I dreamt quite often of the foods that consciously I just disliked or avoided. Subconsciously, in my dreams, they were expressed with true hatred and fear. It seemed as though half the night was spent dreaming of potatoes that continued to accost me!

I do not know exactly what the nightmares and dreams at such an early age might have meant. I was obviously scared of being killed; perhaps I was afraid that I would be separated from my parents. I must have felt that someone was testing me, that what I did was not good, or that I was inferior to others, especially those of my own age.

On the other hand, it would seem that I felt I did not belong in the same category as other children, expressed through the dream of being able to fly. Perhaps these dreams also revealed that in reality I was trying to cover up my fears by putting on an image. I think this idea of covering up my feelings by putting on an image carried on right up to and through adolescence, particularly when I was beginning to develop anorexia.

It was about the time that the bad dreams began that I went through experiences which, looking back, I realise were sexually abusive, and at the time made me feel uncomfortable, embarrassed and different. It was also around this time that a barrier started to be built between Ruth and me, which grew into real hatred and pain. She was incessantly jealous of the time and attention I received, particularly from my mother. To make matters worse I was very friendly and cuddly, even with strangers, and therefore received yet more attention, captivating people with my blonde curls and green eyes! Ruth's way of handling these difficult feelings was by constantly putting me down and making me feel I was a total failure.

Mostly it was Ruth's attitude towards me and her words said about me in front of other people which hurt so much. Only occasionally would she lash out physically. The time which sticks in my mind was when my mother had dropped the two of us off, along with a school friend, to play crazy golf. I was obviously not wanted and was seen to be a nuisance. As Ruth was taking a sweep at the golf ball, in her frustration and anger towards me, she intentionally swung the golf club in my direction. I collapsed to the ground, my hip bone in excruciating pain. One of the adults on duty witnessed this and ran at speed to my rescue; jumping over a fence and ripping her trousers in the process! I was carted off to Casualty, but there was no lasting damage done.

I felt totally powerless to retaliate, especially through words. Most of the time I felt intimidated and speechless, but at times my anger did build up inside and I would lash out and push her over – once so strongly that I knocked one of her teeth out!

Despite my difficulties and fears, I was a child really full of life and buoyancy. I loved to let my imagination run wild. Even if life was tough at times, I had a strong drive always to see the positive or 'nice' things in life (which the poem at the start of this chapter '*Looking and seeing*', reveals). I enjoyed making up games with one or two friends, but most of all I adored to amuse myself. I made stories up with my toys and I would spend hours sitting in the front of the car pretending to drive it and acting all the daily events of an adult. Day after day I amused myself by painting and drawing. Often I would write little notes or stories and scribble a picture on the back. One read, 'Dear Mummy, I like you and we have had a very happy Christmas'. I cannot quite work out what the sketch on the back was supposed to be, though! Another read, 'Dear Mummy, I love you because you love God'.

A happy memory I have is of saying my prayers with my mother at night. A picture which my godmother had given me hung on the wall beside my bed. I loved to look at it: it portrayed such beauty and love. In it, Jesus is standing with the face of a young child clasped between His hands and three other children beside Him. His eyes are staring into the eyes of the child between His hands.

His look is warm and caring, promising her life. So often I imagined myself to be this child and I really felt that Jesus was taking care of me.

2 | *I DON'T THINK ANYONE WILL KNOW*

Why the hurricane does blow
And the child's heart is cold as snow.
I know she has tears in her eyes
And her mind's filled with despise,
For happiness seems never to arise.

She cries herself to sleep at night
And in her dreams continues to fight.
The battle's long and will not end,
Fate appears to be round every bend,
The path gets yet harder to climb,
'Please God save her in time'.

(Aged 13)

During the last two years of my time at junior school Ruth had moved to boarding school. On the days when my schoolfellows teased me about my eyes, or when I felt self-conscious over reading in class because I was slower and more hesitant than most, I found myself longing to join her despite the struggles between us. I had visited the school on several occasions and wanted to be like the children there, with their smart uniform, brown shoes and straw boaters. I so much wanted to be a part of a large family with lots of children all looking out for each other, rather than just Ruth and me, and it seemed as if the children at this school were a family. I watched with envy the way they all entered the chapel on a Sunday with a partner, in a long straight line. Clutching their hymn books in their hands, they bobbed as they passed the altar on the way to their seats. I longed to be an angelic-looking convent schoolgirl!

When my mother was able to take a full-time teaching job, my parents decided that it would be possible for me also to go away to boarding school, so I sat the school entrance exam. To my delight I was accepted to start the following September.

As the time to begin the new school drew closer, my toes twitched with excitement. It was like the build-up to a grand finale. I received my last project, took part in the school sports, received my Amateur Athletic Association Star Award and performed in my last little ballet show, for which my friend's mother had made us both special tutus decorated with sequins. I was so sorry to be leaving the ballet school, for I loved to dance.

At last the big day came, my trunk was full, the clothing list checked off and we were on our way. Four hours later we turned into the school drive, passing the junior school, the hockey pitch on the left and the grass tennis courts on the right. We followed the car in front to the car park of the senior school with a trail of cars behind us. Children dressed in uniform were dodging between each car. It felt strange to think that I was now one of them.

Each form unpacked their trunks in a different room in the school; my trunk was deposited in the junior dining-room. One of the sixth form showed me up to my dormitory. She led me up a long flight of stairs and turned right, passing a row of about eight washbasins. At the end of the corridor was a small, very steep set of stairs, dark and dingy, leading to an attic where there were two dormitories, known as the 'Archangels'. On the right at the top of the stairs was a small bathroom, and straight ahead were the water tanks mumbling away to themselves.

I was in the second dormitory. I found the bed with my name on it, and dumped my suitcase on top. It was a strange room, with very low ceilings and sloping walls, and the windows were tiny. At the end of each bed was a chest of drawers.

I said goodbye to my father, then set to work unpacking my trunk, placing my bedspread on the floor beside it and loading in my belongings. Each time it was full, I gathered the corners to the centre and dragged it up the stairs to the 'Archangels'. When the last few pieces had been taken up, one of the sixth form came over and ticked off each item on a list. It seemed a tedious and unnecessary job. At lunch it felt strange sitting amongst people of a variety of ages, none of whom I knew. I was very shy and certainly had no gift for making conversation; I did not speak until I was spoken to. Then one of the sixth form asked me my name and age. I told her, explaining that I had been ten years old two days before. The only other piece of information I could offer was that I had an older sister called Ruth in the school.

After lunch I met the matron, who welcomed me; 'It's nice to see you with us at last, Helena. I felt quite proud to be one of the new girls and was so pleased that Matron had noticed me.

Our classroom was at the far end of the school block, commonly known as the Barratt block. It was opposite the music practice-rooms and next to the cookery room. I found a desk near the front and put my pencil case, ink and some paper inside it. There were very few desks in the room, as there were only about twelve girls in the class. It was a class in between the junior school and the senior school, known as Lower Remove.

I settled in very quickly and at first did not feel at all homesick. I did not really feel out of place either, as I knew the building and some of the staff through visiting my sister. Ruth had also told me a lot about the routine of boarding school life, so I knew just what to expect.

The lessons did take time to get used to. Many of the subjects were new to me, and most of the other girls had either been to the junior school attached to this school or had covered some of the work before. I began to get rather left behind. My confidence diminished as my work was returned with large red crosses through it and endless circles round words which were incorrectly spelt. I had been taught a method of reading at my previous school which concentrated on the sound rather than the spelling of words. I remember during my first term at boarding school, the headmistress set us an essay entitled 'A nonsense story'. The comment at the end of my essay read, 'Some good nonsense here, Helena, but some of your spelling is nonsensical too! Try very hard to improve it'. I was forever being told that my ideas and imagination were good but my grammar extremely poor.

It was not long before several of the girls in the class started to tease me. I do not know whether this was because I was the youngest in the school, because I had an older sister, or because I was the ideal person to pick on, being very quiet and too scared to tell anyone I was being bullied. To begin with, they just teased me over my work and hid my uniform so I was late for lessons and was told off by the teachers.

Later in that first year two other girls arrived who were equally shy and gullible and they also became targets for bullying, although I remained the chief one. In the morning, either my school shirt or my shoes would be hidden. I would search all over the dormitory for them, with no result. The only thing I could do was to put on another shirt, either next week's (which was a different colour) or my games clothes. Whatever I wore, Matron always noticed and sent me back upstairs, saying I could not have breakfast unless I was dressed properly, so I often had to start the day not having eaten. The girls frequently messed up my school work with ink blots, so I was criticised by teachers for untidy work. If I cried it made the situation worse for it showed I was weak and a good target, so I learned to hide my feelings and only to cry at night. Sometimes Matron would ask me if I had been crying but I did not have the courage to say yes or tell her the reason why.

The effects of being told off by my teachers as a result of being late, not properly dressed or having untidy school work was beginning to make me feel as if I was never good enough and desperately misunderstood. Little did I know that the bullying would get worse and have even greater detrimental effects upon me. Probably the most damaging thing emotionally was being encircled by a group of girls in the dormitory who put me on 'trial'. They were the 'judges' who had to 'try' me. Standing in the middle of them, feeling both fearful and vulnerable, I would be given a series of questions to answer. If I gave the wrong answer then there would be a physical punishment. The trouble was that each question had no correct answer and so all answers were wrong, which meant that a punishment would follow every one: being kicked in the stomach until I vomited, having my head hit against the wall, or having compass ends stuck in my back and the skin torn.

At night the girls told ghost stories to frighten me, and made apple-pie beds. When it was lights out I would leap into bed and either put my foot through the sheet or have to curl up and pretend to be in bed, remaking it after Matron had switched out the lights. One girl in particular used to take my bedspread and hide it, and put powder and soggy tissues in between my sheets. I began to dread the night as much as I did the day.

Looking back, I think the torment and emotional difficulty that came with my first year had quite a lot to do with my developing anorexia, inasmuch as it seriously damaged my self-confidence and destroyed all feelings of being valued. I think that events such as these are contributory factors as they lead to unhealthy self-criticism, a feeling of worthlessness, emotional problems and depression. Eventually these climax in stress. As a friend once said, 'Stress is like the pressure building up in a bottle, and unless it is let out gradually then the pressure becomes so great that it cannot remain inside the bottle any longer, resulting in the cork shooting off and the contents flying out: it explodes'. The results do not show immediately; the build-up is gradual but has a drastic effect.

I longed for something to happen to bring an end to the bullying, someone to do something. Then one of the chief bullies was expelled and I thought it was all going to be fine, but it still carried on. I began to feel increasingly that there must be something wrong with me for the other girls to dislike me so much. I began to blame myself, concluding that I was a useless piece of material that had been rejected by all. There seemed no way out. One of the girls had said that if I told a teacher then I would be killed, and others said that it would prove I was just a coward. I did not want either of these so I kept quiet.

As time went on I began questioning why I had been born and started to conclude that perhaps everyone would be better off without me. I felt so incredibly unhappy and trapped that I decided I would have to do something. I hid behind the curtain at the end of my bed, put my hands around my neck and tried to strangle myself. I squeezed tighter and tighter, but soon my arms ached and I gave up. I couldn't even die properly!

Ruth had already told me that bullying was bound to happen and that it had happened to her. I felt that it would be no use my trying to talk her into helping me. Besides, if I went and cried on her shoulder I would be showing my inability to defend myself. I wrote to tell my parents that I was unhappy and hated my class, hoping that they would take me away from the school. Being the younger sister my letters always had to be sent in with Ruth's, and when she read what I had written she said I could not send the letter to my parents as it would hurt their feelings too much. They had decided to send me away to school and were paying a lot of money for my education, and the girls in my class were bound to leave me alone sooner or later. She told me to tear up the letter and write and tell my parents that everything was fine. I tore up the letter and started again, giving the impression that I was coping.

At the same time I made a vow that I would not tell anyone about how unhappy I was. Instead I learned how to hide my feelings: a disastrous thing to do. I entered a fantasy world, pretending that I was an actress. It no longer mattered if horrible things happened to me because I told myself I was just acting and I had to take the part of someone being hurt – if bad things happened to me it was not real. My dream was that one day I would be in a play where good things would happen and I would be treated like a queen.

So I decided there was nothing I could do about the bullying other than push it aside and enjoy all the other aspects of school life. 'Popularity isn't everything,' I told myself. I was chosen as goal-shooter for the netball team, which really pleased me (especially considering that my sight was only a quarter of most of the other girls in my class). In addition I found my piano lessons exciting; I enjoyed the touch tapestry that I was doing, and I began to get some good marks in lessons. My morale was very much boosted when I received a commendation for a short essay. Once again, the fighter inside me decided to focus on the positive things.

As I was rather young for the class, and to consolidate my learning, I stayed down in the Lower Remove for another year, along with the two girls who had arrived a term late. It might have seemed a shame to stay down but at the same time it was a great relief to see the back of most of my class. I was no longer the youngest and I knew exactly what to expect as far as school routine and lessons were concerned. I could play a dominant role, showing the new girls what to do. I no longer felt pushed around, but in command, and I made some good friends.

We had a new form teacher whom I liked very much. As I had done most of the work in the previous year, my marks began to improve but the teacher also gave me confidence because she encouraged my love of art and acting. She seemed to have confidence in my work, which boosted my morale.

Among my class friends I was happy, although still very timid. However, I found myself living more and more in the imaginary world I had created. It was partly my love of acting and partly my need to aspire to a different world from that in which I was living, where I could be the person I wanted to be rather than the person I was forced to be. I used to make up stories and act them out with one or two friends. We often went out on to the hockey pitch where we had space to imagine that we were on the vast prairie as the characters in a television series.

As I was continually pretending to be someone else my parents' idea that I might like to attend a drama summer school greatly appealed to me. This was an exciting new adventure. In the blazing sun, on the huge lawns of the drama school, set in the beautiful Worcestershire country-side, we learned many aspects of the theatre. Fencing and judo were new techniques which we developed alongside the more familiar acting and dancing. There were two real highlights of the course: the coming together of the different age groups for the filming of *Julius Caesar* and the end-of-course stage production. In this I was chosen to take the lead, a fantastic experience, especially in the setting of the drama school's stately building. As a result of this holiday I decided to drop my piano lessons and take speech and drama as an optional extra at school.

These lessons became a delight to me as the bewildering new school year got underway. Larger classes, new subjects and a form mistress I was frightened of – along with several new girls in my class – shook my earlier confidence. But to try to cope with these feelings I threw myself into what I did enjoy. Some sports where becoming more appealing to me. I joined the gymnastics club, and began taking part in the BAGA awards.

School life was becoming more and more busy, which helped to take my mind off my feelings. I also enjoyed it when annual events came round, as again it gave me something to focus on. One such event, and perhaps my favourite, was Harvest Festival. It was lovely to think that autumn had come, that the harvest was over, and most of all that food could be collected and given to those in need. I loved to help decorate the chapel at the convent, ready for the service on Sunday morning. The headmistress would ask for volunteers to help, and we would load up wheelbarrows at the school with fruit and flowers that had generously been given. The window-ledges and sisters' choir stalls in the chapel would be decorated in the most artistic fashion possible. As one entered through the door at the side, a fresh, fruity smell would waft past. The combination of fruit and straw really made harvest come alive.

Gradually, I began to come to terms with the large classes and various changes. Although nervous and self-conscious, I began to find my feet.

3 | IT'S GETTING DARK

It's getting dark
As the sun sinks low;
The moon doesn't shine
Nor do the stars glow.

My mind is a mirror
Of a saddened world;
My pain a secret
Never to be told.

I am but a child
Whose heart is bleeding;
Affection is the food
That I need feeding.

(Aged 14)

The transformation from child to teenager produced dramatic changes in my feelings and attitude towards life, changes which took place over a period of several months, not simply at the appearance of my first menstruation.

In the August of my thirteenth year, to my great delight, we had our annual holiday in Majorca. This was our second holiday abroad as a family and it was embarked upon by us all with eager anticipation. The location lived up to our expectations. The hotel was at the end of a deep inlet of crystal-clear blue water. Too soon, however, I was aware of an agonising pain in my abdomen and although the lunch menu was tempting I had no appetite. When we went upstairs to unpack I realised that I had started my periods. I was dumbfounded, although I knew all about puberty and was not disgusted. However, before menstruation actually began I had given little thought to the subject, and the gap between childhood and adulthood had seemed very large, with changes far into the future. I could not imagine these things happening to *me*, or *my* body being that of a mature woman.

I told my mother and she put me at my ease instantly, so in some ways I was pleased to be venturing into a new phase of life. The sea and sun relaxed me and as a family we had great fun swimming far out to boats moored in the bay, searching the clear waters with goggles and snorkel for coral and spiky sea-urchins, going for walks along the rocky headlands where we could pick wild figs and almonds. For a short period it seemed we were united as one happy family.

Back in the usual humdrum world of school, the changes in my body and mind became more evident. Although relieved that I was normal, I feared growing up because I felt that I was not ready to face the pressures adulthood would bring. I was happy to be a child and had no reason to change or lose my simple way of life. Growing up threatened my security.

Many of the lectures at school on puberty and sex had been interesting and yet also threatening, because I feared that such things would be forced on me before I was ready to cope. I was too wrapped up in activities such as sport, dancing and drama to take any real interest in boys and had no desire to be sexually appealing; at times the thought almost disgusted me. My changing body also heightened my awareness to the fact that the experiences I had had in childhood were sexual and not just something that made me feel uncomfortable. As I thought about these, and current experiences, it filled me with revulsion which reinforced my thoughts that there must be something profoundly wrong with me. Other girls in my class seemed only too keen to start relationships with boys, but I felt unbearably awkward and terrified that they might 'expect things from me'.

I had also started to feel very conscious of my shape and appearance and extremely sensitive to other people's comments about either clothing or slimness. In many respects I felt content with the shape of my body, which was slim and not very well developed, although at times I felt clumsy and too broad and I longed to be petite and short. I had no desire to increase in weight but neither did I have any reason to weigh myself, so I rarely stood on the bathroom scales.

My classmates frequently attempted to slim, and in order to join in I occasionally announced, 'I'm going on a diet tomorrow', with little intention of carrying it out. It was more an adolescent reaction to having overeaten that day, and never lasted more than a couple of days because I knew there was no need to restrict myself. It is true that I later became self-conscious of my waist and thighs and occasionally grumbled about my large ribcage, but I made no real effort to become thinner.

But teenagers are under tremendous pressure from both the media and their peers to keep their bodies slim. Every magazine I opened was urging me to lose a few inches from my waist and thighs, telling me that life would be more wonderful and that I would be more desirable if I had the ideal figure. Some people in my class said that I had one of the best figures in the group whilst others were highly critical. The pressures of the group, at times, would override my own knowledge that my healthy appetite and physical activity balanced one another well. Confusion and indecision reigned in my mind.

The new-found feelings which arose at this time brought with them fear, confusion and depression, resulting in bizarre eating habits and periods of lack of appetite, as well as a tremendous need to be noticed and loved. It was as if something clicked out of place at times; almost as if there was a fault in the body mechanism which led to the secretion of some substance producing obscure feelings which were, in themselves, a warning sign that anorexia was underway.

There were times when I felt an agonising sense of loss, such as a child might experience whose whole family had died suddenly in a car accident. An inner pain would sweep through my whole being in an intense longing to love and be loved, despite the knowledge that my family dearly loved me. Perhaps it was this, combined with an inability to communicate my innermost thoughts to friends, that made me frequently wish I were someone else. I felt hollow, lonely and lost; an emptiness surrounded me which needed to be filled. It seemed as though others were complete but there was something missing with me; I was the lost and lonely soul on the outside. The feelings would change dramatically, and for no apparent reason, to a mood of happiness in which I was bouncy and relatively self-confident. Then just as suddenly I would become sad again, shut in a world of my own.

These feelings led to a deep sense of insecurity and inferiority which in turn led to extreme sensitivity. I felt that I was worthless compared with others in my form and my sister, who was taking so many O level subjects that seemed out of reach to me.

As my feelings of inferiority grew so my inability to interact and communicate with others increased and I found myself needing to be noticed, not just as a member of the Lower Fourth, one of 28 thirteen-year-olds, but as an individual with my own needs and aspirations. I even found myself being sent out of lessons for not concentrating or for being disobedient, which was not in my nature in the least but was obviously a good way of attracting attention. I half dreaded, half longed for the moment when I had to see the teacher at the end of the lesson, to come face-to-face with her as a person. The ridiculous thing was that normally I was such an obedient child, scared to do anything wrong. The 'click' had produced a new being who would do even this to be noticed as an individual, and yet all my life I had been loved even if, looking back, I can see that some of my emotional needs were not being met and the development of my identity and individuality was disrupted by the way we interacted as a family.

As the academic year progressed, in most people's eyes I had fewer and fewer reasons to be unhappy, yet my unhappiness increased. I was doing well in lessons, improving my grades steadily. I was walking away with five-star pentathlete awards, I had passed the top BAGA award for gymnastics, and my speech and drama Grade 2 examination with merit – yet endlessly I sought attention as though I was trying to say, 'I might have achieved these things but what am I like as a person? Who am I? Please look at me and tell me what the real me is like. On the outside it all looked OK, but on the inside I felt emotionally paralysed.

4 | IN SILENCE

I sit in silence,
Wondering where
My love should lie;
Or does it
Sit in silence
And quietly die?

I sit in silence,
And think of
Stolen years,
My eyes
A gentle stream
Of dew-drop tears.

I sit in silence,
A changing world
Before me blowing!
In my heart
Love and pain
Together flowing.

I sit in silence,
Alone and staring
At an empty sky;
Confused, lost
I ask myself
Who am I?

(Aged 19)

The search for my own identity and difficulties over relationships were the two main features of the next year, and I believe they both played an important part in my developing anorexia. The problems encountered in relationships extended from home to school and were doubtless connected.

In different ways I seemed to struggle with each member of my family. The most obvious battle to others was no doubt the relationship with Ruth. The conflict I had felt in the past grew in such a way that by the time I reached my teens I felt that Ruth regarded me with disdain. It seemed that nothing I did or said was acceptable, and I began to feel that I was simply some brainless insect, good for nothing. The more I longed for her approbation the less I was likely to receive it. It seemed I was a nuisance, and almost always unwelcome. When in her presence, especially at school, I felt intense pain and anguish.

Perhaps Ruth and I should not have been at the same school, making life difficult for one another. The whole idea had been to bring us together after our earlier years of jealousy and fighting, but it seemed to be having quite the opposite effect. One of the sources of our clashes was probably her mistaken idea that I was favoured at home, a natural assumption for, with all my hospitalisation and inability to sleep, I had needed my parents', and in particular my mother's, attention. Perhaps my mother should have left me to scream or drawn Ruth into the situation more, or perhaps my father should have taken Ruth off and played with her more often to give her the feeling that she was equally important, but it is easy to have wisdom after the event. Whatever the answers, her child-understanding could only see a pampered little sister who seemed to receive more love; a deep hurt and bitterness developed which led to great unhappiness for both of us.

There were, at times, little glimpses of another side to Ruth, a side that perhaps others saw more than I did. It was as though, during these moments, she really cared and was proud to have me as her little sister. Like the day she spontaneously bought me some of my favourite sweets: I can still picture myself standing in my grandparents' kitchen, reaching up into the cupboard to tuck them behind a cup so that I did not eat them all at once but made them last! I so longed that we could be friends every day.

The relationship with my parents at this time was, in comparison with many other teenagers, reasonably good. However, it was not without its difficulties. These were not particularly obvious to the outsider, nor even to my parents. In my head I knew they loved me and I loved them, but I felt that there lay a barrier between us. This barrier was probably due to many things. Part of the problem was the way I felt inside as I moved into the adolescent years: I felt distant, angry and as though I was fighting to be *me* and not them. I found my dad to be unemotional and avoiding conflict, when I longed for him to be affirming and able to face problems and deal with them. I felt awkward around my father and repulsed by him at times. He represented male demands. My mum seemed too emotional to be able to cope with my sharing anything in case I overburdened her. She often seemed too tired or too stressed, and I lived in fear (from things that she said) that she was seriously ill and was going to die. She also seemed to live her life through me and I felt like her clone, not an individual. The way she related to me made me so often feel as though we had a joint identity which I hated. I felt like screaming: 'I'm different!' So much pain and anger were bubbling away inside me, but being unable to articulate my feelings I could not explain why I felt so bad.

It seemed that there was little closeness between my parents and there was an atmosphere of tension which rarely left. I longed to be free from the tension and the guilt I felt as a result of living in an environment where

doing and saying the right thing appeared more important than having an open and honest relationship.

I knew that my parents had had problems in their
marriage, to a greater or lesser degree, from very early
days. Moving to Kenya immediately after they married
created difficulties for my mother who was not accustomed to the Kenyan way of life, did not find it easy to
live on a research station, and did not know how to spend
the hours of such empty days. Then having two children
was not the bed of roses perhaps she had hoped it to be –
especially when I came along! Moving to England was a
strain for the whole family, in particular for my father,
who left behind a good job and a country he loved. When
after a matter of months, we found somewhere to live and
he had another job, I know it did not match the work he
had enjoyed so much in Africa. It was clear, too, that there
were struggles between my parents; to me, they did not
seem particularly happy together or able to communicate
or show love towards each other. It hurt to see the difficulties and feel the atmosphere which so often existed
when they were together. I felt it very acutely and took
upon myself their pain, feeling that it was my responsibility to do something to make it better.

At boarding school, being a long way from my parents
in miles, I felt equally far from them in terms of communication and personal contact. By not seeing them for
extensive periods I no longer felt a part of them as I had
done before, and therefore did not feel able to express my
inner feelings to them. I felt distant from them, as though
I was on the end of a string, but the string had knots in it
and I was unable to pass those knots; they kept me away.
I needed the security I found in my parents, yet the need
for independence overrode this much of the time, especially at school.

Because of the feeling Ruth had that I was the favourite,
I pushed against my parents, inwardly rejecting them, in
a determination to prove her wrong. I hated myself for

Ruth's misunderstanding and for being, apparently, the cause of her unhappiness. Therefore, I suppose, in many ways I tried to avoid forming a deep relationship with my parents, for it would mean a worse relationship with Ruth, for whose love I so much longed.

The saying, 'Sticks and stones may break my bones, but words will never harm me', did not apply to me in any way; it was the words and consequent emotional pain that left a scar, not just in the relationships at home but at school too.

That year I had a very deep scar left as a result of broken friendships in my class. I had just made good friends with one of the girls, Michele. Although completely opposite in personality, we shared many of the same interests and understood each other well. Unfortunately, in becoming friends with me she broke off her friendship with another girl. This girl had never liked me and was determined that the last thing I was going to do was to remain friends with Michele. She made it clear that I was the one who had destroyed their friendship and that I was now hated. Whenever I walked into the room I sensed that my presence was very unwelcome, and I was usually greeted with a scornful or sarcastic remark. In her eyes everything that I did was no good: my work was useless, my appearance untidy, my figure far from perfect and my clothes did not suit me. I was generally down-graded the whole time. The strange thing was that just before she left, two years later, she turned to me for help and reassurance, and we developed quite a good relationship. It is interesting how things can change

On one occasion I had been hurt by the same girl's remarks and I refused to go into the biology lesson. Then I came to my senses and told myself that my work was not going to suffer because of someone else's unkindness. I walked in, a little tear-stained, but could not concentrate on my work and instead wrote a poem.

The teacher was fully aware that I had not been concentrating on the lesson, and that this was not the first time; in fact, she had already spoken to me on more than one occasion about not concentrating on my work because of being upset. She did not shout at me, merely asked to see me after the lesson had ended. When everyone else had left and I was standing alone in the laboratory a sudden fear came across me and the words that I so wanted to say were tied round my tongue and refused to break my lips.

'Are you all right?' she asked.

'Yes,' I replied.

'You're not unhappy, are you?'

'No'.

I heard the word 'no' resound in the empty room and there was a deathly silence.

'You're shaking,' she commented.

I wanted to tell her exactly what was going on, my difficulties and my new-found feelings, but she was a teacher and I felt that there was a barrier between us. This was a bad impression to have, because teachers should be concerned with the whole welfare of their pupils and I believe it is very important that pupils feel able to discuss their problems. Being bashful did not help; I could not bring myself to say anything to her.

I wrote a lot of my feelings down on paper and found they were closely related to what people thought of me, in particular teachers, especially if they showed any sign of caring or concern for me. At the end of the year I burnt all my notes in the fear that they might be read, especially after being teased by one of the girls in my dormitory for being one of the teacher's pets. The same teacher often used to talk to me after class.

I remember on one occasion there had been tremendous rivalry over friendships, and the situation had got out of hand. As usual I was the centre of the problem, and one of the girls had been extremely spiteful to me. I arrived late for the lesson feeling as if the world hated me, sat by myself and forced the tears back. I could not see the blackboard so did not write any notes. When I received my preparation back, it read '2/10 – rubbish'. On top of everything, I was experiencing my first bout of real depression. By the time it came to the practical of the biology lesson, I could not take any more and walked out of the lesson into the cloakroom. I had worked myself up into such a state that I was physically sick.

The teacher fetched me and spoke to me privately after the lesson. I managed to explain the situation over friendships, my worry over work and exams and feelings of depression. She soon put me at ease and said that if need be she could sort out the trouble that I was receiving from the girl in my class. She was concerned about my work and noticed that when I was unhappy my marks dropped dramatically, and this in itself was why I received low marks. She reassured me that there was no reason whatsoever to worry over my exams.

I remember her saying I worried about trivial things, and also that my failing was comparing myself with others.

On the surface I portrayed a totally different image to that of the insecure child within. Several people had commented on how mature I was for my age: not physically, intellectually or the way in which I acted, but in the form of self-expression and sensitivity. Rather than joining in with the fun and games of adolescence I would prefer to express my inner feelings and thoughts on a subject through prose, poetry or art.

As a result of adolescence and the problems over relationships I found myself on even more of a desperate search for my own identity. I began to question the value of my own existence. In reality I knew who I was, that I was a living human being, yet I constantly asked myself, 'Who am I?' I had to find out what I was actually like as a person before I would be able to live life to the full. My search went on and on through the everyday happenings of life and in the quiet of the night, as I tried to discover who I *really* was: what I was *really* like deep down inside when the mask was removed; what reason I had for living; to whom I belonged; who I loved; who loved me. I wrote in my diary:

'Why don't I fade?' I ask myself. 'Or have I faded?'
'Can people see me as I really am?'
'Can I see myself as I really am?'
'How do I know what I should really be like?
'My heart floats in the air, it belongs nowhere.'

In my search for identity the creativity within me played an important role. Through acting and poetry, painting and dance, I found that I was able to begin to catch a glimpse of that being which was myself.

5 | DARKNESS IN MY MIND

Darkness in my mind
An endless black hole
That extends to eternity;
Deep and daunting.

Numbness throughout my body,
Dead, all feeling postponed,
Too heavy to rise;
Limp and lifeless.

(Aged 19)

My world was drowning in waves of depression and I was sinking into a deep hole; the muddy earth began to cave in on me and my vision was clouded. The falling earth pressed upon me, hammering me deeper into this fearful dark hole. The waves lashed around me; I was drowning in my own emotions.

Another disastrous lesson had just finished. I felt a tear trickle down my cheek, and bit my lip, forcing back all evidence that I was upset.

As I was packing up my books and leaving the room at the end of the lesson, the teacher called me to her.

'What's wrong, Helena?' she asked.

'Nothing.'

'It's no good saying that. Come on, I want to help you and listen sympathetically.'

I told her that generally everything was getting me

down. The lunch bell went in mid-conversation, and she suggested that we made a move towards the refectory.

'I don't want anything to eat,' I said.

'Don't be silly,' she replied in a quiet but firm voice.

'I don't want any.'

'Come on now, Helena, try just a little, just the pudding.'

She took hold of my arm gently and I went to the refectory with her. Grace had been said and everyone was seated. A profound fear flowed through me and the smell of the food made me feel sick.

'I can't, I can't,' I protested.

'Come on, I'll find somewhere for you to sit.'

'No, no. Please, I don't want any.'

The thought of sitting down and eating was enough to terrify me, but in the end she sat me at a table. I ate very little and felt very sick.

That afternoon the situation came to a climax. In the history lesson we had been given permission to do some private reading. Nothing was said against doing school work as an alternative so I decided to finish my English prep. Suddenly the silence was broken by a harsh voice.

'What do you think you are doing, Helena?'

'My English prep,' I replied in a very subdued voice.

'You deceitful child.'

'Sorry,' I said very apologetically. 'I didn't hear y——'

'Are you deaf as well as all your other disabilities?' she shrieked back at me in a cruel voice.

My eyes filled with tears, I felt a great pain come over me and my heart started pounding with the teacher's last remark. There I was, struggling to overcome my difficulties and be like any normal child, and she gave the impression that I actually enjoyed having something wrong with me. The bell rang for the end of the lesson and tears surged forward. I dried my eyes as one of my friends, Frances, came over and asked if I would like a game of tennis. I said that I would rather just sit for a few minutes but if she went and booked the court then I would love to play in half an hour.

However, the history teacher turned to me and said in a harsh voice, 'You can get out of here now.' That was the end. I left my books, got up and ran down the stairs, out of the building and on to the hockey pitch. I sat down by an old log and cried and cried. Frances came over to me a short while later.

'I hate it here, I really, really hate it,' I said, the tears streaming down my face.

In the background I could hear music from the senior common room; the song being played was, 'All by myself'. The words sank painfully into me as the singer spoke of not wanting to be all by himself any more; not wanting to live feeling insecure. It was like a thorn piercing my heart.

My only means of coping with these feelings was through prayer, and I started to go to the early morning chapel service twice a week. I believed in God, but my belief had no real meaning and my prayers no depth; I simply knew that I had an inner need and found myself drawn to that place of peace and serenity. Somehow it gave me the inner strength that I needed to cope with life. During the silent moments I thought a lot about my paternal grandparents whom I had never known. Grandpa had died before I was born and Grandma never lived to see my third birthday. It saddened me that I had not known them whilst they were alive, yet I felt a strange closeness to them, especially Grandma, as though she was with me in all I did and understood my feelings. I knew them as people far better in a spiritual sense than I could have known them in an earthly one. I loved them and they loved me, and I knew they were with me through both the good and the bad times.

I hardly knew my father's side of the family; all I knew was that I felt a part of them. I felt the same closeness and family link to one of my cousins, Kathie, who was 17 years older than me and lived in Bermuda. Late one night I sat on the edge of my bed feeling desperately unhappy and wrote and told her. I had rarely spoken to anyone of being depressed before, because it was a new-found feeling that scared me and that I did not know how to describe. I thought that, to an outsider, being depressed for no apparent reason must seem ridiculous, and it must all be in my mind. Kathie told me in reply that it is normal to get depressed; the problem is trying to find the strength to overcome it, and we all need other people to help us. She described how our teenage years are the worst ones to get through because so many changes are happening to us, physical, mental and psychological. It is a time when we are questioning every aspect of life, because we are trying to mould our values for the future. She ended by saying it is how we learn to cope with our problems that is important.

The new realisation that I was going through a natural process made it easier to cope with my problems and new-found feelings.

I hoped, having gained the knowledge that these feelings were part of life's experience and a step to maturity, that their intensity might lessen; but this was not to be. Although the new school year brought changes – our O-level subjects chosen, new teachers and new girls, dormitories over the other side of the school and freedom to walk to the local village in groups, my fifteenth birthday and two Duke of Edinburgh Silver Award Camps – I fell quickly from these heights into my dark hole.

During the two days of walking and camping for the Duke of Edinburgh Award I found I could not eat, and lived off apples and dried milk, not even bothering to hydrate it. Emotionally I felt dreadful: I had landed in the hole with a mighty thud. I stumbled in the darkness, falling over my own feet. The hole extended into a tunnel; either side of me and above was a wall as dense as one could imagine. At the far end was a small opening through which light was escaping, but it was too far in the distance to crawl to, let alone stretch out my hand and feel. I tried to ease myself back to where I had fallen in; I stretched my hand back to feel for the entrance, the empty space extended to eternity and when I turned my head there was not even a glimmer of light to be seen.

6 | MUDDLED EMOTIONS

Won't you tell me how I feel,
Whether my heart's made of steel?
For it seems so cold and hard,
Even battered and scarred
Yet I simply don't know
If I'm riding high or low.

Do I feel with my heart or head?
Is half of me alive, half dead?
If only someone would say,
For I hate living this way,
On an island devoid of land,
With emotions I can't understand.

(Aged 15)

People, people overwhelmed! Wherever they might be, in any situation, as the feelings of inferiority filled me and I felt degraded and useless, so people swamped me. Yet at times I would walk on air, held in the heights of joy, only to descend dramatically to the lowest depths. There was no intermediate stage, no middle road, no slow descent.

The pain in my mind would rip through my whole body, not pain as in a cut finger but an inner torture which yet was physical. Tearful and lost, my inner soul in torment, my whole being seemed to shriek for peace and stillness, contentment and serenity.

I needed to talk to someone and I longed to be with

Kathie, but thousands of miles of sea were between us, and although she had told me to ring her whenever I needed to there were too many problems over doing so. Out of desperation I gave a note to the cookery teacher. Doing this was totally out of character: I did not like to show my feelings and was far too bashful to explain how I felt, but I think this was a real cry for help. I scribbled, in haste, on a piece of paper:

Please help me.
I can't stand another minute. Please don't tell anyone but the pressure of depression makes me feel sick and unhappy, and I hate the sight of food.
I can't stand any more; I thought you'd understand how I feel but if you think I'm stupid just tear this piece of paper up and say nothing.

As I approached her with the piece of paper I thought I must be mad. She had already told me off once that day for not eating and said that she did not want me to fade away. As she pulled her bike out from under the shelter, I handed her the piece of paper.

'What's this? It's not my birthday,' she said jokingly, and started to open it.

'Please don't open it until you get home.' I said goodbye and dashed inside. At least the situation was off my chest, if nothing else.

The next day I received a letter from my other cousin, Sue, whom I had not seen for seven years and even then only briefly at her wedding. It was lovely to hear all her news. And that afternoon my restless mind was put at ease when the cookery teacher came up to me and said, 'You come and see me some time.'

After lunch I went along to see her. She was busy showing someone her wedding photos and afterwards she showed them to me. She pulled a chair towards her desk and told me to sit down.

'What's it all about, then?' she asked.

'I don't know,' I said, stuck for words.

She understood, and told me that we do not always know what exactly it is that is upsetting us.

'I think you worry too easily,' she added, and asked what I was worried about.

'Work, I guess,' I said.

'There are far more things than work, Helena. What else?'

I told her what had been on my mind recently. Then she asked about my parents and sister and went on to talk about tension and depression. She said that I was in a deep hole and needed to climb out, but would be unable to do this alone.

At that moment the class bell went, but she said I would have to miss the next lesson and she would explain to the teacher where I had been. We went on to talk about jealousy and friendships and she advised me what to do.

'Sit at the front, smile and try to be happy, Helena.'

I sighed.

'Do you know what I expect of my pupils, of you, Helena? To work hard? That's not the most important thing. Enjoy yourself, be happy!'

Just before I left I gave her one of my poems and told her about not being able to eat.

'Of course you can't eat,' she said, 'because your stomach is all churned up, but try to eat a little.'

I went through quite a long spell of not wanting to eat and avoiding meals. Food seemed both a friend and an enemy: sometimes it comforted me and at other times it accosted me. If for any reason I was upset or under pressure I tended not to eat, partly because I was not hungry and partly because the control over my appetite made me feel I was in command, which boosted my morale. At times I really hated the sight of food; it sickened me. On other occasions I had hunger pains but no appetite; my stomach craved food but my mind was not interested.

On one occasion I sat down at the dinner table and

asked if I could have a small helping; I just toyed with it and when the sweet arrived I refused it. Someone on the table commented about my aversion to food and said that she thought I had got anorexia or 'AN' as she called it. I knew very little about anorexia and adamantly denied the suggestion. However, I was reported to Matron for not eating, and as a result had to sit next to her at mealtimes for several weeks.

It was around this time that I had more eating problems when staying with a school friend. I enjoyed the easy-going lifestyle of the family, but the thing which marred my stay was the fact that they tended to eat rather large meals composed mainly of stodgy food, and I found this increasingly difficult to cope with. I felt guilty over the amount of food that I was consuming and often suffered from a bloated feeling and bad indigestion. Several months previously I had found that foods high in fat both nauseated me and gave me indigestion so I decided, where possible, to cut them out of my diet. Obviously, over the months, my body had been accustomed to a fat-free diet, and being laden with foods that it was not used to produced a negative reaction.

Having cut down on some foods I began to feel guilty about eating, not because I was on a strict diet with the intention of losing a set amount of weight, although I was concerned with not passing 8 stone, but because I considered that I was losing my self-control. It felt that if I lost my control over a trivial matter such as eating, then I would lose my control over myself, and I would therefore no longer *be* myself. I was constantly threatened: as soon as my self-control slackened I sensed a take-over bid from the impinging world. I was no longer who I was; my 'self' had been snatched up.

Some girls had noticed my erratic eating patterns. One day the cookery teacher stopped me in the corridor.

'People have told me about you not eating,' she said in a concerned voice.

I looked down, feeling rather awkward and embarrassed.

'Is not being able to eat upsetting you a bit?'

'Yes'.

'Unless you start to eat there'll be a lot of letters, and you wouldn't like that, would you?'

'No'.

The tone of voice suddenly changed. 'I loved your poem, Helena. You should take it up professionally'.

'Thanks', I said, quite taken aback.

'Do you want it back?' she asked.

'No, you can keep it'.

I had thought that my unhappiness and depression would have eased a little, having been able to talk to someone, but I was mistaken: each day became more clouded, my anxiety increased and I became frustrated and at times resentful. To make things worse I developed a rash on my chest and eczema on my arms and back. At night I lay awake tossing and turning, unable to sleep. Worse still, there happened to be scabies going round the school and I was unfortunate enough to catch it. I was staying with my grandparents when it started to develop and my grandmother was very kind. She took me along to the doctor, painted the liquid remedy on and generally took great care of me.

It was lovely to see the Christmas holidays arrive. It had been a long dark term and I was looking forward to going home again. For once I really enjoyed myself, whereas usually I felt just as depressed at home. But a terrible time lay ahead.

I returned to school with exams on my mind. I could not get down to revision, I could not concentrate, and I seemed too tired to work for any length of time. It was more of a mental fatigue than a physical exhaustion, and I found myself breaking down very easily. I felt as though I was in battle with myself. It was a subconscious, continual battle, and as it progressed so the outer me, the visible me, became frustrated and miserably dejected. If only I could have recognised what the inner me was fighting over and why. My brain could not register exactly what was going on. It was a strange feeling which left me in a helpless, isolated, dark world. Others stood in the light, yet I was trapped in the dark. I stretched out my hand so often to pull myself through, but back I would be pushed, landing with a mighty thud, as though I was a worthless being. The whole world disappeared from me: I watched it shrink into the background, becoming smaller and smaller. The more I was pushed down, the more I lacked self-esteem; and the lower I was pushed, the greater the need to succeed and the desire for achievement became.

The following description is of a picture that I painted at the time.

Isolated from the outside world, I am living in it, breathing in it, but I'm trapped. A transparent shell surrounds my body, barricading me from all its beauties; such beauties I see but can't reach. I stretch forward, but my hand collides with the membrane; I cannot feel what my eyes see, I hear the melodious sounds but they don't penetrate. On one side of me there is food; on the other, water. I long to take them, but I can't.

As my confusion and unhappiness deepened, the more my sense of insecurity grew. I did not know where to turn and I felt a great sense of loss and grief, as though something very deep was missing. It was at these moments that I sat and thought about my cousin Kathie. I thought of the stories that she told me in her letters about going to stay with Grandma and Grandpa every summer, and I wished I could escape to the world she wrote about:

It was like going back in time a century, with all the photos of our ancestors on the wall in the hallway, the summer-house in the garden and the orchard in which Grandpa gave us our own apple tree. I can still picture him carving the Sunday joint, sitting in his armchair at the table, and going to the shops with me and Rusty, the dog, who could do just about anything. It's a pity that you didn't know Grandpa; he was a wonderful man.

As I read what Kathie had written to me it all felt so alive, and I felt so much a part of the family. It was as though I had been searching for something precious and at last I had found it. In many ways I had. I was searching for my own identity and I had found the roots of it, for although I am my own person, my traits lay here, in people I did not know.

Whenever Kathie wrote of the 'family' it made me imagine myself a part of it and reinforced a strong desire I already had to be in among a big family with brothers and sisters all sitting round a large wooden table, sharing and caring. Instead, it felt as though I had ended up with a sister who hated me and parents who did not appear close. So many times I sat and wept, 'If only I hadn't been born then no one would feel hurt'. Most of the essays I wrote at school were about a young child being rescued and taken care of, or a child who was in a children's home being chosen by someone to be adopted. My stories were so convincing that my English teacher queried at the end of one whether it was true! I fantasised and day-dreamed so much; each dream took me to a world where I was looked after by an adult, but where I could be free to be myself and was blissfully happy.

With all my day-dreaming and fantasising I was not at all surprised to find out that I had done badly in most of my school exams! My results were not bad enough to be referred to the headmistress, but being disappointed by my comparatively low marks I decided to discuss them with her. She said that I had obviously worked hard, but I did not realise the big jump between Upper Fourth and Lower Fifth and that she did not doubt my ability to do well next time. Then she went on to say that I gave her the impression that I was lonely, and she told me that I was too thin.'

Just as I was leaving the room, the biology teacher walked in and the headmistress asked her if I was supposed to have seen her to discuss my results.

'No,' was the reply. 'But I know she's thinking life isn't worth living right now.'

During the previous biology lesson, the teacher had told me that I was capable of the work and the only reason my exam results were worse than usual was because I was depressed. She was too right!

Although some of the teachers were obviously noticing the change in my mood and weight, no one seemed to step out and help. Perhaps they themselves felt at a loss as to what the best thing would be to help me? I longed for someone to understand and to know what to do about the situation. It left me wondering if anybody could do anything. 'Maybe I'm the only one in the world who feels like this, and no one can help me,' I thought to myself.

7 | LEARN TO LIVE

People should learn to be themselves,
Why pretend to be someone else
Acting life on the wrong stage
Just to create a pleasing image?

We all have a pre-set scene
Our futures can be foreseen,
And there's an individual path sown
If only its format could be known.

So upon our paths we must stay,
Conquering every obstacle in the way,
Learning to live our own life,
To battle on and overcome strife.

Creating a better being within oneself,
Not looking for alternatives on the shelf.
The wrong road leads to the dark
Where life hasn't even a spark.

It's uncanny, cold and bare,
With a sense of isolation out there,
Living in another's shell
Where such confusion can dwell.

So forget all the sadness you feel,
A little happiness learn to steal,
Live the person you're meant to be
And a new life you'll begin to see.

(Aged 18)

To compensate for the less attractive aspects of life, I held in my hands certain precious gifts which I released at times when I needed to let my inhibitions fly away. Once more I made an attempt to focus on these positive things rather than the struggles and difficulties in life.

Writing, art, dance and drama have always helped me to release my pent-up feelings. Since early childhood, writing has been my solace and means of expression: right from the time in infant school when we wrote our illustrated news books, through the stages of making up little stories and long newsy letters home with lively little sketches incorporated, to a very special writing relationship I had with Doris.

Doris is the mother of one of the older girls, Mary, who was in the sixth form when I first started boarding school. Although a great deal older than me, Doris was, and still is, a great friend. I came to know her when she and my grandparents both moved to the same town. We kept up a frequent correspondence, writing just about anything to each other, from school to politics and war to fantasy. We shared the same interest in writing and a keen appreciation of life. Many times I wrote to her reflecting on my inner feelings. Most of the time I did not write because I felt I wanted to: rather I felt compelled to in order to release my thoughts, ideas and feelings. When I wrote I did so in a mature manner, and so while I would sometimes write of pain I could not let her see the desperation and the childishness I felt inside in case it robbed me of the relationship: we were on an equal footing and I could not change that relationship to one where she 'looked after me'. I was only too grateful to have someone who could respect my need to write and appreciate my letters. It was through being free to express myself and through what Doris said in her letters that I realised the importance of finding oneself. When I was 16 I started to feel an even greater sense of the need really to be myself, as Ruth had left school and I no longer lived in her shadow. Doris obviously had the same thoughts over the matter as I did. She said in a letter:

> Actually I think it's a good thing that you're coming here on your own for half-term and I think that now Ruth has left school you may feel less tense. This is no reflection on Ruth or you, but I think it's not always the right thing for sisters or brothers to be at the same school, as each is often living in the shadow of the other. I saw that with some of my own children and in my own case.

In our letters we quite often discussed depression: what causes it and how to cope with it, how one can be depressed for no apparent reason, and the connection between depression and the need for identity. Doris said in another letter:

> I think some of us live more deeply than others. We can achieve greater heights of happiness and real joy – but at the other end of the scale we can reach depths unknown to other people. When I see something breathtakingly beautiful, I can *feel* its beauty, and my heart leaps with joy. I savour these moments when I am experiencing something of real meaning. When I feel down, I know it'll pass and I try to turn to something that I know will give me joy. That's not easy and not always possible, but do remember the feeling will pass.
>
> Thank you for writing – go on writing and writing. I do believe it's a way of finding oneself, and some people can put on paper what they can't put into words; the spoken word is so nebulous and intangible.

The aspect of English which I enjoyed most at school was writing essays. These enabled me to use my imagination and I would often find myself writing essays for sheer enjoyment on deeper subjects. In my early boarding school days I wrote some short stories among which, naturally, was one about boarding school life and, more unusually, a fantasy called *The Time Eater*. By the time I was 14 I had also written my first book, following the death of my sister's dog, Minky – in pencil and for my eyes only! But the writing which at the time gave me most pleasure and helped me to unwind was poetry; art was my other passion. Often I would illustrate what I wrote.

To stand alone in the light, airy art-room with its large windows overlooking the ever-changing shades of the leaves on the trees, paper in front of me and paintbrush or pencil in hand, became a source of tranquillity and inspiration, my relief from emotional anguish. On looking at the finished article one begins to understand the depth and content of one's own feelings. If I have a blemish on my face, I feel it and wonder what it is; it is not obvious. But on looking in the mirror I can see clearly what it is. So with the painting: that which was only half apparent and hidden in the depths of my being would be there for me to see on the paper. I had a better understanding; I felt cleansed and the frustration would be gone. Art was an excellent way of coping with my feelings, even if only for a limited period.

When I received my O level design paper with two weeks' preliminary studies to do, there were several questions which I could have chosen. After much thought I decided to design the scenery for a setting of a play which was trying to convey the idea of modern soullessness. I thought I must be mad to have chosen such a difficult question, as no one else attempted it, but my art teacher was delighted that I had made that decision; she had very much liked the only other stage-set I had done. From the moment I started to work on the design I derived great satisfaction from it, firstly working on the theme in sketch form for the preliminary studies, then explaining in writing how the idea evolved and sketching out where the scenery would be placed on the stage. Then the backcloth was designed and finally I did a painting of the view that the audience would have of the set.

Through working on that design many of my tensions and inhibitions were relieved. This made my school work in general far easier.

Dance was also one of my greatest delights. In the rigid structure of ballet and tap-dancing lessons there was a challenge and discipline which were both demanding and rewarding. I found exhilaration and enjoyment in the shows we did in some of the neighbouring small towns, and there was always an air of fun and joy on the occasions when we danced out in the open air, at village and church fêtes.

Besides dance, the other times I felt most satisfied were during my speech and drama lessons. I frequently chose to recite poems with themes to which I could relate, so that rather than just reciting them I could feel what the poet was really trying to convey and become a part of the poem. It is perhaps interesting that for my Grade 3 examination I chose the poem *Hunger* by Laurence Binyon. My tutor said that I read the poem beautifully, with great meaning, and the examiner commented that I had tremendous force in the last line, which spoke of 'being' hunger. At the time I did not know the irony of choosing this poem, but now I am sure it must have been a cry for help. There were plenty of times when I said I was not hungry and was unable to eat, and yet my body craved food. I really experienced the agony of hunger; the pain must have registered in my mind.

As my speech and drama lessons progressed, acting began to replace poetry as a form of self-expression. Once again I chose parts to which I could relate, and in which I could become emotionally involved, so that I experienced the feelings of the character I played. This also enabled me to give rein to my own feelings. The soliloquies from plays which I acted, either in preparation for an examination or for one of several school drama evenings, gave me an inner satisfaction far greater than that achieved in taking part in a complete play. This was partly because I always chose the intense or heart-rending speeches which ended on a climax.

Two of my favourite pieces, which I performed on separate occasions, were a speech of Olga's from Anton Chekhov's play *The Three Sisters* and Saint Joan's speech on being condemned, from Bernard Shaw's play *Saint Joan*. To my immense delight my performance of Olga brought much praise, in particular from the headmistress and English teacher, but it was the part of Saint Joan which gave me the deepest sense of fulfilment. As I sat in front of the audience, curtains parted, I was filled with great fear, something which did not usually happen (a few nerves maybe, but not fear). For a split second my mind was filled with a jumble of thoughts. I felt that I could not go ahead with the part; I would have to leave the stage. I felt as though I had been sitting there speechless for an eternity. Suddenly my fear burst into the intense words of Saint Joan. I leapt into a standing position; chains around my ankles – Joan, the prisoner!

8 | *ILLUSIONS*
OF REALITY

I have seen the mirage
Freeze and crack
That once reflected
The ray of light,
Appearances that comprise reality.

Green hills have faded
Into the distance,
Covered by sheets
Of drifted snow
Intertwined with the dull grey sky.

Trees are faint
And flicker in the darkness;
The wind is but
An eerie lull
And birds have no music in their hearts.

Words that I have
Long believed
Become engulfed
In the mist
And fade into invisible air.

The stream flows
Down to stillness
And dissolves
In the uncanny sea
Enlightened by the sinking sun.

(Aged 18)

There were so many positive aspects to my life and in some respects good happenings, in addition to the bad ones, in the time leading up to my O levels, that in some ways it is surprising that there should have been such a dark battle going on within my body. It was as if my inner being was under attack. I was being torn asunder. I felt as though I was stranded on a barren island, but even that started to crack beneath my feet. I was totally confused as to why I felt such heartache and agonising emotional torment. I was at school without Ruth and achieving well in my lessons. I was no longer in a dormitory but shared a study bedroom and I had the freedom of the nearest town at weekends, if accompanied by two other girls – not that that was much compensation. An American acquaintance once said to me about that town, 'It's half the size of New York Cemetery and twice as dead!'

I felt an unbearable, aching loneliness. My inability to communicate with my class companions grew daily; I could not reach them, nor did I feel a part of their world. My confusion over life grew, and the waves of depression became even more overwhelming.

A climax of unhappiness and depression had built up and in desperation I wrote a letter to the problem page of a teenage magazine. It was more to relieve the pressure than anything else. A short time later I received a reply.

Dear Helena,

Thanks for your letter. I think you should seek professional help because obviously you have a serious problem here. Go to your doctor as soon as possible and tell him all about your worries, just as you told them to me. Make sure you explain fully about the depressions and headaches, and ask him if he thinks he should refer you to a psychiatrist.

Now, I know that sounds pretty drastic and please don't think I'm saying you're mad! I do, however, think that psychiatric treatment could help you sort out a lot of your troubles, and there's nothing at all to be afraid of. I hope this helps you.

I was relieved when the letter came, but rather shocked when the person suggested that I should see a doctor and psychiatrist. Whilst I was writing to the magazine I did not give a thought as to the reply; nonetheless, I had not expected quite such a dramatic answer. It put me in a very difficult situation, as there was no way that I could get to see a doctor whilst at school unless I told Matron. That meant explaining the problems to her, which I could not bring myself to do. However, I did discuss the subject with one of the young assistant matrons, who advised that I should go to see a doctor. She mentioned that she could arrange it, but would have to speak to Matron and the headmistress first. I said I would rather forget the idea. She went on to say something that has always stuck in my mind.

'You know, there's only one person who can really help you – God.'

I thought of what Kathie had told me in her letter as well: 'The only way you can find the strength to cope with life is through faith and the overwhelming love of God.'

So I decided to cope on my own, and I asked God to give me the strength to do so.

If I had wanted, I could have gone to a doctor at home, but the end of term seemed such a long way off and the odds were that I might be fine by the time I actually got there. Besides, I did not want to say anything to my parents about the problem, as I remembered what Ruth had told me that first year at boarding school: 'You can't tell them you're unhappy. It would hurt their feelings too much.'

From that moment I had decided I could cope alone and I had no intention of causing them any upset. I was also aware that my problems were very much wrapped up in family matters and my past. It was too painful to think about it, let alone say anything.

During the holidays there was a great sense of alone-ness, too, and at times I felt burdened by the bitterness and pain I had tried to keep buried for so long. Being at school away from my parents, and that year from Ruth as well, I had time to think about my bitterness. Why did I feel so distant from my parents even six years later? Why did my sister despise me so much, when all I had done was to be born? Why did I feel so desperately hurt? Even though I thought about all these things, I could not come to any conclusions and the deep hurt remained with me still.

I remember times when I looked into the mirror and saw a dejected face. I felt great pain for no apparent reason – it totally mystified me. I stared and stared into the sorrowful, piercing eyes that seemed to outstare me. I looked down, then once more looked bashfully at this face in the distance, so divorced from me. I watched a tear trickle down the sallow cheek; my heart felt torn with agony – my eyes were red and glowing with unshed tears. I turned away and moved towards the door, then quickly glanced back at the mirror. I was shocked to realise that I was a part of that mystical picture by which I had been fascinated. But why was I crying? I was not upset. No, not upset, but in agonising torment, and I had no control over these abstract and disturbing feelings.

I was working very hard for my early O levels, revising every spare minute of my time. I preferred to work during the lunch break, eating some fruit, rather than go into the refectory for a meal. I found the small-talk at the dinner table monotonous and, although I was hungry, I had no appetite for food. A plateful of meat and vegetables, the strong smell wafting past my nose, was more than I could tolerate.

Towards the end of lunch break, after school or at week-ends, I quite often went over to the junior house to spend some time with the younger members of the school. I love children and it brought me great satisfaction to help them with their hobbies, teach them tunes on the recorder or play duets on the piano. The affection that some of them showed me made me feel appreciated. Perhaps the time with the children was special because I had lost all awareness of being appreciated and loved as an individual, and being with them restored some of this sense. Not feeling loved and valued was, I am sure, a part of why I felt so depressed. Yet rather than facing up to the depression and trying to deal with it, I would turn my back on it and try to deny its existence, convincing myself that it had gone away.

Through observing the simple, carefree lives of the younger children, I longed to be the same – to be able to accept myself as I was and live life to the full. As a member of the senior school it felt as if there were so many pressures. There appeared to be so much emphasis on competition and success. At school and through the media there was the constant pressure to succeed academically and have the perfect figure, but the worst pressure was perhaps the fact that failure in any of these areas seemed to indicate failure as a person: that if your performance was no good, *you* were no good.

I began to believe that unless I was at the top of my class then I was useless. Even when I came first in a subject, I still felt that my work was not good enough – I should have been first in every subject. I perceived this to mean that, as a person, I was not good enough. I watched other people continually come top of the class with little effort and certainly no gratitude, whilst I worked twice as hard to achieve the same.

So much emphasis is laid upon achievement that I feel the values in life easily get out of proportion. We are indoctrinated to believe that our lives depend on the height that we reach on the ladder of success. I think that the desire for achievement can override and even distort our personality. This is particularly significant in anorexia. Some doctors and psychiatrists believe that overemphasis on success is one of the underlying causes of anorexia. I do not entirely agree; I would say that it puts one under considerable pressure and therefore increases the level of stress. It is said that anorexics are nearly always of above average intelligence, with pressure on a high academic achievement from either home or school. Rather than seeing the anorexic rebelling against being the best, I see her striving for perfection, but never quite reaching either her own standards or those expected of her. This results in a lowering of her self-esteem, putting her under even greater pressure.

I soon discovered that in working extra hard, virtually non-stop, and drawing up lists of what I would allow myself to eat, I could more or less hold my depression and unhappiness at bay. I woke very early in the mornings and immediately started to exercise or do school work. I then drew up a chart of what I had eaten the previous day and a chart of what I was allowed that day (it had to be slightly less each day). I took a keen interest in each subject I was studying and directed all my mental energy into lessons, prep and revision. I spent the evenings dancing, reading, sketching or writing poetry. The only way I could cope was to become very disciplined and rigid in what I would and would not allow myself to eat and do. I did not really mind what I was doing, so long as my time was fully occupied and I could push my troubles down. But it was hard to keep my highly disciplined life, as things around me constantly threatened my way of living. As the pressure inside increased I wrote in my diary:

You know every day I have been so tired, depressed and had headaches recently. I know in myself there is something infinitely wrong. Every day it gets worse and I don't understand why. Everyone gets depressed and I did over short periods for about two years, but now it happens every day. I have so little energy and I can't take the pressure of absolutely anything anymore. Why, why, why?

In the Autumn of my O level year I had taken three subjects to get them out of the way, and during this time the standard of the remaining subjects tended to improve as I began to derive great satisfaction from aiming for high marks. The end of term seemed to arrive quickly, but likewise so did the end of the Christmas holidays. Although no one said anything at the time, my mother noticed that I had lost weight around the face and that I was eating a lot of meat and fewer carbohydrates. Ruth noticed that I had stopped eating sweets, desserts and cakes. Quite frequently in my diary I wrote of feeling bloated, sick or not being hungry. Towards the end of the holidays I received my three early O level results: Art, grade B; RE grade B; and to my shame English Language, grade D. I was very disappointed with the results as I had hoped for at least one A and two B's. It gave me the determination to work hard for my mocks and get no less than grade B in any of my remaining O levels.

9 | ONLY THE LONELY

Isolated in an empty space,
No longer can she run the race.
She forces herself to carry on
But all enthusiasm has gone.

If ever she reaches the end
There's yet another bend,
And she turns around
Only to fall to the ground.

Why continue to fight
When hope's no longer in sight?
It's easier to end it there
Than live in deep despair.

With the pills upon the shelf
She's bound to console herself,
Staring with a longing eye
She breathes a heavy sigh.

She looks with deep thought
It's the last resort,
She'll rid herself of strain,
It's so easy, there's no pain.

Peacefully, lying down
Is how she'll be found;
Why she let herself go
Only the lonely will know.

(Aged 16)

To my delight the Easter term began well. I had decided not to worry about the future, nor to look back on the past; I would take each day as it came. I really enjoyed getting involved in my O level work and began to take note of what I was writing rather than just taking down dictation and revising parrot-fashion. Although I felt a lot better in myself, and far more healthy than I had done for some time, at my first tap-dancing lesson the teacher said she thought I had lost a lot of weight. A few days later one of the girls in my class commented that I looked ill. I did not know whether I had lost any weight, but I felt fine. I had taken quite an interest in food and a liking to cookery. I spent hours looking at recipes for a vegetarian cookery book that I was planning to put together for my mother, who a year or two previously had been put on a vege-tarian diet for health reasons. I was becoming more and more of a health food addict.

I suddenly found that in spite of all the mental energy I was putting into my work, I had a vast amount of phys-ical energy. This was a restlessness which became a compulsive need to exercise. A friend and I decided to do keep-fit exercises in the gym each day, gradually building up the amount each session and the number of sessions per day. To begin with I found that the more exercise I had, the more I was able to eat and the less I suffered from indigestion; this, however, was not main-tained. Yet I began to feel that I was in control of myself, for I had managed to organise not only an exercise routine but also my free time and school work. Despite my disappointment over my english language O level result, I began to feel that there was still hope when the teacher told me that it was not my English that needed improvement – in fact my compositions were very good – it was my lack of concentration through being so unhappy which was interfering with my work. My morale was given a boost when I received the first chapter of my O level history project back marked

'Excellent. Well written.' Things were certainly looking up!

During the Easter term I went to stay with my grand-parents for the long weekend break. Since they had some scales, I decided to weigh myself. Towards the end of the Christmas holidays I had noticed that I had lost a few pounds and was 8 stone (already below what I should be for my age and height). This time I was 7 stone 10 pounds. I was pleased that I had lost weight without really even trying. I did not have a set weight I wanted to be, but did notice that having lost weight I had gained a sense of achievement. It felt as though without the goal to keep on losing weight life would once more become too much to bear. I felt pleased that at last I was taking control of my own life and managing to be successful.

When I returned to school I found that the tenor of life had changed. I wrote in my diary, 'I had a bad night and woke up feeling ill. The thought of lessons really got me down and I felt weak all day. I had to do some revision, but I was so tired I lay down.' My fear was that the depression and pain would surface again if I did not keep on the go with my eating, exercise and work plan. I could not afford to be slack!

The same week we all had to be checked by the doctor for scabies, as someone in the school had caught it again. This meant lining up with our shirts off. One of the girls in the class looked at me and said, 'Cor, Helena, your ribs! You must be anorexic.' The doctor did not notice that there was anything wrong with me so I thought no more of her statement.

The mock O levels began a few days later and all my energies were directed towards revision for them. I got up early in the morning to revise, usually around 6.00 am, at times as early as 5.00 am. I would slip my school uniform on and creep down the stairs and work in the library until the rising bell went, when the silence would be shattered. Then after this I would jog round the hockey pitch to get some oxygen to my brain and keep myself fit.

At the end of the first day of mocks I had a tap-dancing lesson and my teacher commented again that I had lost a lot of weight and said I had better not lose any more. A year or two previously she had noticed that I had an eating problem and had talked to me about it. I could not see what all the fuss was about as I did not feel as if I had lost any weight at all. However, I was aware that I was not eating much and quite often missed meals. The next day my speech and drama tutor commented on how thin I looked. Each day I worked non-stop, except for a little food, from 6.00 am until 9.00 pm. Then I would have a cup of herb tea. Almost every night I would go to bed with a crashing headache and feeling freezing cold.

I used to pile layers of clothes on my blue limbs and curl up at the bottom of the bed, yet the cold gripped my body and ate deep into my flesh and bones. I would stuff my ears with cotton-wool to block out the noise from the corridors and other rooms, and very rarely succeeded in getting a good night's sleep. I was always awake and ready to be on the move in the early hours of the morning. My whole sleeping pattern had been disrupted.

One thing that began to concern me a little was that I had not menstruated since Christmas and it was now the end of February. I did not really worry about it, but kept telling myself everything would be all right next month. At my next dancing lesson the teacher once more commented on my appearance, asking how much I weighed. As I did not have any access to scales at school, I truthfully told her that I did not know. Her reply was, 'Weigh yourself before you die.' That scared me, but the feeling soon wore off. I still could not tell that I had lost much weight, despite my clothes having become looser; my perception of size was already distorted. If anything I felt better for having lost weight, not so much physically but mentally.

The day mocks ended, half-term began. No sooner had

I walked into my grandparents' house than my grandmother remarked on how thin I looked and asked me whether I had lost weight. I weighed myself; I was 7 stone 5 pounds. Once more I gained a sense of achievement. I had managed to discipline myself and must not give up now. It was not so much that I wanted to lose weight but I needed to achieve continual goals, and weight loss was one goal which seemed to be both achievable and to work well.

I felt very close to my grandparents that half-term and apart from doing a small amount of work I spent nearly all the time with them. My grandfather had declined rapidly since I had last seen him and I felt deeply for him. He was an extremely intelligent man, and to see the frustration over his loss of memory and his struggle to walk, in contrast to his breathtaking stride of the past, was very sad. Despite this sadness it was an extremely memorable time for me. I wanted to help restore his confidence in himself and so I sometimes played Scrabble with him, ignoring the mistakes that he made and constantly asking his advice to boost his morale. We took short walks in the sea air, his arm securely linked through mine. We sat and talked about various things; he showed me how to do artwork in copper and told me that I should write children's books. I helped my grandmother to prepare meals and sat and talked to her about writing and painting. I really felt that I had benefited a lot from that time with them. The only problem I really faced during half-term was that because of eating fairly normal meals I suffered terrible stomach pains.

With my mock O levels behind me, my main aim was to complete my history project and concentrate on my speech and drama Grade 5 exam, to be taken later that term, as well as working hard for my O levels the next term. As a part of our history coursework we watched *Holocaust*. I found it really interesting, but the brutal, bestial way in which the Jews were treated by the Nazis was agonising to watch and the scenes very much played on my mind. I took such incidents deeply into myself and almost relived the events. I did not know how to separate myself from them, perhaps because of being very sensitive and a deep thinker. As I dwelt on such terrible events I began to shut myself off from others; I could not summon up any enthusiasm for a social life with my school friends. I could not join in with their laughter, my spirits were too low and I did not find what they said funny. My depressed mood had returned and I could not 'snap out of it'; instead my mind wandered off to dwell on hopelessness and despair. It felt as though the world was determined to be against me, and I cried tears of confusion all alone. Once again I decided to concentrate hard on my studies, filling my spare time painting, exercising and planning what I would allow myself to eat.

I had started to pass out, especially during and after games lessons. I tried to keep this secret and where possible avoided hockey lessons by asking if I could play badminton instead with a friend. This was a lot easier, especially when we talked for some of the time, and sometimes I missed the lesson altogether. Once when I felt faint in the middle of the lesson, the teacher sent me to Matron, who dosed me up with glucose. She told the teacher that I had been working too hard, but the teacher insisted that it was more than hard work and said that I had lost about two stone and looked very ill. I was so cold and dizzy that I could not bear to go into lunch that day; instead I got into bed to keep warm and ate an orange. Fruit was about the only food that I could tolerate without a feeling of revulsion or nausea, and I virtually lived on it.

I knew I had to keep going until the end of term, despite having begun to feel desperately ill. The vast amount of energy which I had had at the start of the term had vanished, and my dancing was the only exercise that I could manage to keep up. I frequently felt drained, my head heavier than my body, and I was continuously cold, a coldness that sank deep inside me. My limbs were worst affected; they had a constant purple colouring. I could see that I looked tired and drawn, but not that I was thin. When I looked in the mirror I saw plenty of flesh. I did not feel particularly thin, and as far as eating went I kept my difficulties as well hidden as I could.

My form mistress stopped me in the corridor and asked if she could see me alone. I had dark rings under my eyes, my cheeks were sunken, my school uniform hung on me shapelessly. I felt terrible. She said that I looked very pale and thin, that I was like a shadow and advised me to be sure that I ate enough and did not work too hard.

After lessons, nine of our class were going on a retreat at the guesthouse, a part of the convent in the nearest city. Earlier I had received a phone call from my boyfriend, Andy, saying that he was coming up to see me that weekend. We had been friends since we met at drama summer school when we were both 11. When I was 14 he asked me out and since then we had seen each other during the holidays. I felt very self-conscious and awkward; I wanted his friendship but going out seemed so strange. Never once had he asked to see me at school and I knew that his turning up was something the school would frown upon. I explained that I was on retreat and that he could not see me, and hoped that he had got the message!

We arrived at the guesthouse in time for supper, but as usual I was not hungry and simply toyed with my food. We were sleeping on camp-beds in the hall next to the guesthouse. It was a freezing night and I was so cold that I felt physically sick. A friend gave me her blanket as she was warm but even so the cold crept deep into my bones.

I had been looking forward to going on retreat all term and the second day began well. We had a helpful talk on posture and prayer and then had our own little Communion service in a tiny chapel in an old hermit's cell. We all went back to the guesthouse for coffee and sat singing folk songs to the guitar. Then we had lunch, and just before the end I received a message that there was someone to see me. As I walked along the corridor my heart thumped. I hoped it was not Andy; we had shared some happy moments and I did not want them to be destroyed by me getting into trouble. I opened the door and there he was. What on earth was I going to do? He had travelled about 150 miles by train; how could I send him back straight-away? I asked the RE teacher in charge if Andy could come to the university with us in the afternoon and to my relief he said he could. When we arrived back at the guest-house I had to tell him to leave. I felt bad about the whole episode.

The following day was an absolute disaster. It was a Sunday and our last day on retreat. We walked to church and then returned to school by mini-bus. It was near to lunch-time when we arrived, so we put our bags down outside the refectory and started to tell the others what it had been like. Matron came over and told me in a stern voice that the headmistress wanted to see me straight-away and that she was not in a very good mood. I thought that it had to be something to do with the retreat weekend and I timidly walked into her office. It was. Everything had been blown up out of proportion. She said that when the RE teacher had reported Andy's appearance, I was the last person she had expected to be involved. I tried to tell her that I had spoken to Andy on the phone and told him not to come but the tears surged forward. She said that she was shocked, and what would my mother think.

She handed me a bus timetable and told me to catch the next bus to the city, walk to the guesthouse and apologise for having a male friend and being so rude. Then I must come straight back to school, walk to the Convent and apologise to the RE teacher and finally report back to her.

I was exhausted. Tears slowly trickled down my cheeks and I was shaking. I had never been to the city alone or even on a bus alone. I had no idea of how to find the guesthouse and I did not know how I would see the bus numbers or even find my way back – I was absolutely terrified. As I was walking down the corridor I met Frances. She asked me what had happened and insisted that she came with me because I was in no fit state to go by myself and she was scared that I might get run over or collapse. I was so grateful to her for offering, but at the same time I was scared that the headmistress might find out and I would be in even more trouble for allowing her to come with me. But Frances insisted. She took my bags to the bedroom whilst I put a jacket on, and then we secretly walked to the bus stop. There was a bitterly cold wind and we stood at the bus stop for ages, freezing. I had no gloves and was only wearing a thin cotton dress and jacket. Eventually we reached the guesthouse, and I knocked on the door. One of the sisters opened it.

'I'm sorry,' I said.

She asked me what I was sorry about, and I explained the incident at the retreat. My eyes filled with tears and I was shivering with cold. She put her arm round me and said that she understood and I was not to worry about it. When she realised that we had come all that way she asked us to come inside and gave us some lunch. For once food felt really welcome. She told me to put everything in the past and take care going back to school.

When we arrived back I went and apologised to the RE teacher, who said he hoped I had learned my lesson. I then reported back to the headmistress. I was completely exhausted. I made my way up to my bedroom, opened the door and collapsed on the floor. A friend came into the room and went to fetch one of the assistant matrons, Anne, who helped me onto my bed and put a blanket over me whilst she ran a hot bath. Afterwards she gave me an aspirin and made me lie down until supper-time.

'I'll pray for you, Helena,' she said.

I wished that I could have had handfuls of aspirins and taken them all, so that I could have slipped into a deep sleep and never woken up. But like the whole of my life, I was trapped: I could not get out to buy what I needed to go to sleep and end the nightmare, nor did I have the courage to step out and do something. Instead, I just entered my fantasy world about being found limp and lifeless and someone coming to rescue me.

When the bell rang Anne told me I had better go into supper even if I ate nothing, but I had better come back to bed straight afterwards.

Later on in the evening I said that I wanted to ring home to wish my mother a happy Mothers' Day. When my mother asked how the retreat had gone, I said that it had been a disaster and told her what had happened. I had been looking forward to that weekend all term, as it was time away from school and I thought it would renew my strength and help me to feel at peace, but instead the weekend turned out so differently. I forced back the tears as I explained about having to go back to apologise, and how cold and ill I felt. She was furious and upset that I had been treated this way but unfortunately did not realise how ill I was. She rang the RE teacher to find out more and complain about the harsh treatment. He said nothing whatsoever about my physical state, commenting only that he had given Andy permission to be with us and that his behaviour and mine had been perfectly satisfactory. She then rang the headmistress, who also said there was no problem. So why did they treat me so harshly?

For the next two days I was still very ill and found it almost impossible to concentrate on lessons. The thought of the end of term being a few days away was the only thing that kept me going. One evening the headmistress called me to her office. She said that I looked very thin and pale, that she had never seen anyone lose weight so quickly and if I returned to school looking like this next term then she would send me home straightaway. Then she went on to ask me about how half-term had been and how my grandparents were, whether I had heard from my mother and how she was. It turned out to be a very pleasant chat and she told me not to work too hard, and make sure that I ate.

In my last art lesson that term, I completed an imaginative composition I had been working on for the past few weeks. The art teacher said that it was very good and asked me to put my name, age and title on the back because she wanted it put into the Ellingham Mill Art Exhibition. I called the painting 'Inescapable Loneliness'. I did not realise at the time that a lot of my feelings had been reflected in this painting.

Lessons were coming to an end and the end of term spirit set in. When the last night came a group of us wrapped ourselves up in blankets to keep warm and watched the Academy Awards in the television room, then we all gathered in one bedroom and sat talking by torchlight. Everyone kept on telling me that I looked terribly scrawny and needed to put on weight. Two of the assistant matrons walked in and said that they would turn a blind eye to the fact that we were not in bed so long as we were a little quieter. At about midnight they came in again and suggested everyone went to bed.

We had the end-of-term Eucharist and Assembly, and then my father came to pick me up. I was so pleased to see him; I just wanted to get home as quickly as possible. He was shocked at how ill I looked and remarked that I had lost a lot of weight. When we arrived home my mother was horrified at my appearance and feared that I had leukaemia. It was lovely to be home and in the warm. My parents read my school report, which was very good, although at the end the headmistress said I had been working very hard and worn myself into a shadow. But during the term there had been no calls to my parents saying that the school were worried about me in any way. Both my parents felt shocked and let down.

During the holidays my energy level was decreasing and I felt extremely lethargic. To begin with, my parents were at work and Ruth was at college, so I studied, still feeling the pressure to do as well as I could in my exams. One Saturday I wanted to buy some more clothes and went into town with my mother. She was horrified at how thin I was when she saw me undress. When we arrived back home I was so tired that in the middle of one of my favourite television programmes I went to bed. My mother came upstairs and asked me why I was so tired. She thought it best to check on what my weight was: I weighed 6 stone 10 pounds. I lay down again, drained of energy. Her eyes filled with tears and she voiced her regret at not being able to care for me, so far away from school: 'I thought I was doing the right thing,' she sobbed.

To help me relax she gently massaged my back, but was in for even more of a shock when she found that not only were my arms and legs covered in hair but my back had a line of fine body hair on it. My mother at the time knew nothing of the symptoms of anorexia and, though saddened by the sight, had no idea that it was linked with my state of health.

We were meant to be going to Italy a few days later and my parents decided that I must see a doctor before we left. I went to a naturopathic doctor who gave me a medical check up, said that my liver was out of sorts and advised that I kept to a raw food diet.

Ruth had finished her term at college and we were spending more time together and were far more compatible. The day before my parents and I were due to fly to Italy, while Ruth and I were sitting listening to records and talking, the telephone rang and she dashed to answer it. When she came back upstairs her eyes were watering and I knew there was something wrong. She told me that our grandfather was unconscious in hospital; he had suffered a massive stroke. My parents came home and rang up to find out how he was – he was in a coma. The immediate reaction was to cancel our holiday, but we were all in need of one and knew that Grandad would want us to go and would be upset if we missed it because of him.

Early on Maunday Thursday we flew to Naples and travelled to Amalfi, where we were to stay for a week. The scenery was beautiful and the change welcome. Good Friday brought a wonderful experience. In the evening all the houses and shops had fire torches outside; a procession of all white-hooded figures carrying a coffin came down the steps of the cathedral and through the streets; behind, there was a man in tatty clothes and bare feet carrying a cross – Jesus. Following was a band and singers. The scene was very moving and I felt very close to God.

We had a lovely time wandering around Pompei, going up Mount Vesuvius and visiting Capri. I was eating reasonably well but felt really cold the whole time. Towards the end of the holiday we received a telex to say that my grandfather had died during Good Friday night. My mother was obviously very upset at the loss of her father, but we knew that it was for the best.

We flew back to England, ready to travel up to the cremation very early the next day. I had an appointment with the naturopathic doctor first, who was pleased that I had managed to maintain my weight whilst on holiday. He suspected that I had anorexia and put me on a special diet. Neither my parents nor I could believe that I had anorexia because I had not been slimming.

My grandfather's death was only the second I had known and I felt an inexplicable loss. I was not deeply upset, because I knew he had not suffered and that there is life after death, but I felt a strange emptiness. I helped arrange the flowers in the church and we had a beautiful requiem service. I knew that my grandfather was at peace.

I was due to return to school that week. My parents had already spoken to the headmistress and it had been decided that I would be a day girl, living with my grandmother, so that she would have some company and I would be able to keep to the diet more easily. There had been so much tension during the past week that it was difficult to eat even the smallest amount and food really nauseated me. I had dropped down to 6 stone 7 pounds, which was well below average for my height.

My mother was still staying the day I returned to school, and as it was a Friday, my half-day, she planned to pick me up at lunchtime. I travelled in with Veronica, next-door, who taught at the junior house. I could not concentrate in the lessons at all and if anyone asked me anything about the past I broke down. I was freezing cold and by the time my mother came I kept on having to go to the bathroom because of the laxatives the doctor suggested I take for constipation. I went back to my grandmother's and it was decided that I should have a second opinion over my symptoms.

I went along to a local GP who said that she wanted some blood and urine tests done at the hospital. My mother drove me over to the hospital and sat with me whilst the blood was being taken. My pulse was weak and the doctor found it difficult to obtain any blood. He kept moving the needle further into my vein; suddenly my head felt heavy and I passed out. I did not know where I was when I first came round; I was lying flat, my mother and the doctor crouching over me. The nurse brought a glass of cold water and I stayed there a little longer before we drove back. I felt completely drained of all energy and my head still felt very heavy and dizzy. On the way home, we called in to see my friend Doris. She laid me down on the sofa by a warm log fire and brought me some sweet lemon tea – my body craved sweetness in order to keep it going. It felt as though even the reserve glycogen supply in my muscles had been depleted.

The blood test came through: I was a little anaemic but it was not leukaemia, which was a relief to everyone. However I was not well enough to return to school. It was decided that I would study at home and return only for the exams. I saw the teachers concerned, who told me what to concentrate on. The cookery teacher very kindly rang up the Board to find out whether I could be assessed, so I left a medical certificate and some model answers in case they were of benefit. They all wished me a good recovery.

I worked on my studies at home, friends popped in to see me and I was reasonably content. I had no appetite whatsoever now, never felt hungry and constantly felt nauseated. I was losing a pound a day, still exercising and feeling increasingly guilty if I ate. I went to see my own doctor who sent me for yet more blood tests and a chest X-ray. The blood tests proved negative, the lung fields appeared clear and there was no evidence of tuberculosis. When I returned to the doctor he said that he was referring me to a consultant physician at the Royal Berkshire Hospital. I was beyond caring now, I just wanted to find out what was wrong and to feel myself again. The days dragged on slowly; I began to feel that I could not go on much longer. At last the day to see the consultant physician came. He checked me over, asked a few questions about how I felt, then spoke to my parents and finally to me, saying that I had to drop my O levels and go into hospital to be treated for anorexia nervosa.

10 | IN SEARCH OF HAPPINESS

Lost in a world of sorrow
Can I see the prospects for tomorrow?
Seems the pain will never go.
Someone help me very soon
Before happiness is doomed.
Let me live my own life,
One of joy not of strife.

Somewhere down deep inside
There's a love I cannot hide,
That love I know I need to share
With someone who will always care,
Of gentle spirit and kind of heart,
Then happiness will never part.

(Aged 14)

At 9.30 am on Thursday, May 15 1980, at the age of 16, I was admitted to the Royal Berkshire Hospital. I had previously been told that I was being sent to the medical ward which nursed people with various diseases. I imagined a room with perhaps ten beds, people of my own age and a little older, a day room with a television and a chance for visitors to come and sit peacefully and chat. The room would be clean and clinical with a tranquil atmosphere, only the murmur of nurses' voices and tapping of feet along the corridors. I think my notion was misguided, as from the minute I was admitted things were not in the least as I had expected. I was taken past a row of beds occupied by motionless bodies, the smell of illness oozing around my heavy head. I found myself in a room isolated from the rest of the ward.

Before I had a chance to be accustomed to my new accommodation, I had to change into my night-clothes and sit on the weighing scales. I watched a graph being pinned above my head which I presumed was to monitor the progress or decline, as the case may be, of my weight. There certainly was no delay in the arrival of the doctor. My parents were asked to leave and I was left with the doctor and the nurse who had just weighed me. The door was closed, the windows shut and the light above my head switched on. He proceeded to open up his case. I feared the worst and wished I could disappear. I was not in the mood to be poked and prodded around. First they took my blood pressure with me standing up, then with me lying down. While I was lying down they drained more blood out of me, took my temperature and pulse along with a few other tests, spoke some medical jargon and told me I would be visited by another doctor in a short while.

At midday I was served a plateful of half-cold food covered by a metal lid, which I cautiously lifted up. The drifting smell that escaped made me feel sick and I just pushed it aside. Shortly afterwards the dietician paid me a visit, clutching a clipboard with various pieces of paper attached. She looked down at one of the sheets of paper and explained that everything I ate had to be carefully recorded and the calorific value for each day worked out, increasing the calories to between two and three thousand per day. I was to be put on a high-protein, high-calorie diet as the energy available from my previous diet was insufficient to meet demands and the amino acids were being used as a source of energy instead of building new body tissue and controlling chemical changes within the body cells. If this were prolonged it could have adverse effects upon the blood and vital body organs. She went on to mention that ideally she would like an hourly feed of 'build-up', a milk-based liquid.

It was not long before one of the nurses came along with a bedpan and asked for a urine sample, then confidently went ahead with taking my temperature, pulse and blood pressure again. I had only been in hospital for five hours, yet I had already begun to feel like a test-dummy – things constantly pumped in and out! The consultant physician came along and talked for a short time, mentioning that I would be put on a drug called chlorpromazine, otherwise known as Largactil, a sedative used to enhance the appetite and prevent nausea and vomiting. However, I later found out that it is in fact a major tranquilliser used for treating psychoses and behavioural disturbances, and I had no idea of the problems it can cause. Having explained what medication I would be put on, the physician said that he would be visiting me once a week on his rounds, but one of several house doctors would be checking up on me daily.

'Peace at last!' I thought to myself after they had all left. I was absolutely exhausted and in desperate need of some sleep. However, I discovered even on the first night that sleeping for any length of time in a hospital is an almost impossible task. I fell asleep the minute my head hit the pillow, despite the noise and the fact that the lights were blazing, but the next thing I was aware of was being woken up by a stranger. It was the staff nurse, with the medicine trolley of all things! Trying to sleep again was hopeless: the crashing and banging from the sluice, ambulance sirens in the distance and various unidentifiable noises swirled around my throbbing head. What is more, I was freezing cold and I can never get to sleep when cold. So I became restless, trying to find a position in which I could best conserve the heat, blot out the noise and at the same time try to think pleasant thoughts to take my mind off the depressing surroundings. Presumably aroused by my restlessness, a nurse soon appeared at my bedside.

'Are you all right, love?'

I looked at the shadowy figure by my bed. I could just make out her face by the light thrown on it, shining through the gap in the door.

'I can't sleep and I'm cold,' I whispered. She fetched me another blanket and sat and talked for a while. Then I fell asleep.

The following morning I was woken up at 6.00 am to be given a cup of tea. My first reaction was annoyance. I could not understand why I was not left to sleep. However, I felt consoled when the same nurse came and talked to me until the changeover shift. Naturally the starting conversation had to be my illness. She mentioned that previously there had been a little girl suffering from the same condition on this ward who walked out a happy girl, full of life, but it took a couple of months of intensive treatment. I could not help but think, 'I only hope I don't have to be in this room for a couple of months, it would be unbearable.' The subject, to my relief, soon changed to hobbies and interests, and we discovered that we shared a love of dancing.

As the sun rose it shone on the flower poster I had beside me, lighting up its delicate petals. I read a few pages from the book *Appointment in Jerusalem* by Derek Prince, and was actually convinced that bad situations can be turned around for good. This idea did not last long though. I was suddenly gripped by an overwhelming sense of loneliness. My light, which I had tried to keep burning, became shaded by darkness that extended into a thick grey cloud.

The hours blurred into days. I was still isolated in that small room surrounded only by four walls. The routine of having my blood pressure, temperature, pulse and weight recorded became monotonous. I was managing to take some solid food, but it continued to nauseate me and my weight still fell. I could not read more than one page of a book without my concentration being impaired. If I were to stand for any length of time I felt drastically heavy-headed and faint due to the high dosage of Largactil I was being given three times a day. I began to live only for the visitors who came to see me. They were the highlights of my day, but my lack of concentration made it difficult for people to stay long.

After about a week of being separated from other patients I was taken into the adjoining ward to make room for a woman with an undiagnosed disease requiring complete isolation. I walked alongside the sister into the large ward. Everyone was a lot older than me and I felt very uneasy. The sister showed me to my new bed, number 27, quite by coincidence the same number as the cot in the hospital where I had been born!

A little while later a young girl of 15, only a year younger than me, was admitted into the next bed. I soon discovered that she was called Helen. We began to exchange information about our illnesses. For several months she had repeatedly suffered from fevers, headaches and weakness. The doctors thought she had glandular fever but because they were not totally convinced she was brought into hospital for further investigation.

11 | *On the water's edge*

My body's a piece of seaweed
On the water's edge,
It rises and falls
With the tide.

The lashing waves tear me
On the jagged rocks,
They throw me up high
And beat me down.

A rejected lifeless weed
Swept on to the shore,
Helplessly I shrivel up
In the burning sun.

Throw me back into the sea,
Help me feel the water
Pass into my body
And give me life.

(Aged 18)

My first night in the main ward was terrible, far noisier than the previous room, and the moaning of ill people was most disconcerting. I lay awake watching the nurses check up on the glucose drips at odd times, observing them change the bags for the lady next to me who was having a blood transfusion and watching other people being taken off or put on saline drips. There appeared to be more activity at night than in the day!

Having had such an unrestful night I woke up feeling even more tired. I do not think Helen had had much sleep either.

'Is it always as distracting as that during the night?' she asked. 'And do they have to wake you up at 6.30 am?'

'Fraid so!' I replied. 'In a few minutes the auxiliaries will come round with a bowl of water and draw the curtains round your bed so that you can wash.'

Sure enough they did. We were shut off from one another by curtains but that did not prevent us from carrying on our conversation. It was a real consolation to find someone else whose O levels were having to suffer due to illness. Helen was not quite as unfortunate as I was, as she was not in her O level year, but the subjects she was taking early had to be forgotten. I had taken three early, but the remaining five, and four CSEs, had been ruled out. In expressing our anguish over such matters we both felt a lot better.

After breakfast the house doctor I had seen when first admitted paid me a visit. He was young and much easier to talk to than a lot of the other doctors. 'He has a good bedside manner,' as one of the nurses put it.

As he approached the end of my bed he looked at my medical file, then peered up at my weight chart.

'Hey, your weight chart's going the wrong way. I wouldn't like to see you fall off the bottom!'

He looked down at me and smiled, then walked round to the side of my bed. He turned to the chart again: 'You know, when you come out of hospital you ought to paint that chart; it looks rather like mountains, don't you think?'

I nodded my head, feeling rather amused at the thought. He sat down on the edge of my bed and looked at me with sincerity. I dreaded what his next words would be, since my weight had fallen.

'Last time I came to see you, you had been drawing a

picture. Have you done any more?'

Relief swept over me and I passed him my latest sketch book.

'They're lovely,' he said, glancing through the pages. 'If you are this good now, with extra tuition you could make a good position in the art world.'

I felt quite touched by his last remark.

In the afternoon the same doctor was on his rounds and happened to walk past my bed; he glanced at my weight chart quickly.

'That's more like it,' he said. 'It's looking more like a mountain now!' He smiled and carried on with his rounds.

I could hardly believe my ears. My weight had increased by only 0.2kg, yet he had bothered to comment and had even shown enthusiasm. I was half expecting some sarcastic comment like, 'It's meant to be a mountain, not a molehill.'

I actually managed to eat something that evening, only I had such an excruciating pain in my stomach that I began to wonder whether the effort was really worth the pain and discomfort. I desperately needed reassurance, but the following day the hammer came down on me with a mighty blow. Once again I had slept badly, had woken up with a crashing headache and was feeling considerably weaker. Throughout the day I felt worse and by the afternoon I had gone down quite a lot in weight. I had not had my bowels open for five days so experienced an unpleasant and unsuccessful suppository, followed by a bowel enema. When the staff nurse explained what this was I tried to put off having it as I felt so weak. I simply could not bear the thought of any painful treatment, but I had to go ahead with feeling degraded and having what seemed like the last of my energy drained.

No sooner were the curtains drawn back than one of the less pleasant house doctors came to see me. He promptly sat down on my bed and looked up at my weight chart in a scornful manner. 'Why have you lost weight?' was his first question, asked in a harsh, penetrating voice. He was incredibly tactless and I felt a lump form in my throat. He stood up and briskly drew the curtains around my bed. His hurtful comments continued to shower me and he forced me to drink every drop of the soup that was in my hand. Finally he got up and walked away, leaving the curtains still around me.

Emotionally, I was too weak to cope, I felt my body tense up, and slowly tears rolled down my cheeks. A few minutes later Nurse C. peeped round the curtain. She was a very caring and competent person and I got on well with her. She rushed over to my bed.

'What did he say to you?' she said with compassion.

I told her all that the house doctor had said, that they would stop even visitors coming to see me if I did not get better soon, and how he had made me drink the soup in front of him.

'Take no notice whatsoever; he hasn't got much patience for this illness, I'm afraid.'

At last they put an end to my restless nights. The nurses had noticed that I had not been sleeping and the physician prescribed sleeping tablets. Whilst visiting me he had voiced his concern, as I had lost even more weight that day. My bones felt extra prominent as they rubbed against the sheets and became sore. For the first time I was able to see that I was thin. The nurse had left the bathroom for a few minutes, and on looking in the mirror I saw my whole hip-joint, the rounded bone from my front to my back, but it did not worry me in the least.

The sleeping pills had worked wonders the previous night, but the second night I did not sleep quite so peacefully. I was knocked out five minutes after taking the pills but woke up several times after that. I saw the night sister being taken round the beds by one of the SRNs, who informed her of each patient's illness and progress. I had been awake on several occasions when they had walked past before. The nurse would whisper something about me to the sister, who would nod her head and say, 'Hello,' recognising that I was awake. This particular night I decided that I had better pretend to be asleep; after all I was on sleeping pills! As I lay there, my eyes closed and my breathing shallow, they approached the end of my bed.

'This is Helena, a little anorexic girl. She has been in for several weeks now and has continued to decline. Her condition is serious and they are fighting for her.'

What I had just heard was certainly not what I had expected to hear. I knew I was ill, but was unaware that it had got to that extreme. I was so desperately confused. It was not that I did not want to get better, I just could not get better. I lay there terrified, my emotions knotted up. I honestly did not know which was the better alternative: to try to cope with fighting the battle, or to be defeated.

I went up in weight by 100g the following day and the doctors mentioned that they were aiming for my weight to reach 42kg before they decided whether I was well enough to leave hospital. I looked up at the graph. I was not much good with metric weight and roughly converted it into imperial – it was about 6 stone 7 pounds. I felt disillusioned. It seemed miles to the top of that graph, and surely an impossibility to reach it within the next few weeks. It seemed such a long time until I would be going home. Even if I managed to put the weight on quickly, I still did not feel cured within myself and I would only have a relapse and find myself back in hospital. I wanted to get better, yet at the same time was afraid of getting better; why, I do not know. I think I partly feared that if I got better and left hospital all the tension, pressure and fear would overwhelm me again. I was 'protected' in hospital: no school, no exams, no tension at home and even my boyfriend, Andy, was not allowed to see me because of the pressure of any physical expectations. If I felt bad in hospital, how on earth would I feel out of hospital? I was in a dark tunnel and I did not know which end had the most light; which way should I turn?

I lay there feeling miserable and dejected. The days passed by, marked only by the recurring discomfort of the pain in my stomach and the unease of the monotonous position in bed. My weight had gone up slightly one day but it did not last and the next day I had lost twice the amount. I was totally humiliated. Nurse C. came over to take my blood pressure and pulse. She looked at me with deep concern in her eyes.

'I'm really worried about you now, you're only 5 stone 7 pounds. Young girls of your age have died of anorexia and I hope to God you don't.'

I was stunned; I did not know what to say.

That night something happened that radically changed my perception of myself and gave me the courage to fight. I had fallen asleep a short time before the medicine trolley came round and consequently woke up in the middle of the night feeling severely depressed. I tossed and turned for several hours, crying quietly to myself. I felt isolated and lonely; I could not bear to be awake any longer experiencing these terrible feelings. I rang my bell; the nurse soon arrived.

'Can I have my sleeping pill please?' I asked. 'I can't sleep.'

'Sorry, it's gone midnight and we can't issue them after this time,' she replied.

As she walked away tears flowed down my sunken cheeks; I could not face any more. My body felt icy cold and as though it was sinking deeper and deeper. I felt as though two parts of me were separating.

I sensed that the life left within me was being drained from my body and the hands of Death were firmly gripping me. I had no more strength to fight, no will to live. All I could do was pray to God that His will for me would be done. At that moment I just surrendered to Him the little life that was left and said, 'Lord, if you want me to die, I'll die, but if You want me to live then give me the courage to fight this illness and live.'

I was wide awake and very aware of all that was going on around me. As I looked across at the curtains closed round the bed opposite, I saw a figure in brilliant white, radiating beauty and tranquillity. The figure smiled, which warmed my heart, and the kindness in the eyes filled me with a strange love and peace. (Later, people tried to tell me that either I was hallucinating or that it was the Virgin Mary appearing, but looking back I am sure that it was an angel.) Suddenly my body felt warm and relaxed. I turned over and switched on my tape of Fisherfolk songs that I had been given, and the words which came singing into my ears were, 'Jesus took my burdens and He rolled them in the sea'. I knew instantly that I had been promised life.

I sat up and wiped my eyes. One of the nurses came over to me and asked, 'Do you want a drink?'

'Yes please, I'll have a cup of Horlicks.'

I could not believe what I had just said. I had asked for a milky drink and for the first time I actually drank it all, closed my eyes and fell asleep.

A real flood of joy had entered my heart that night; I knew that the missing piece to the puzzle of my life had been discovered. I felt an inexplicable love and security. For as long as I can remember I had believed in God and needed Him to help me gain self-confidence and find a purpose in the things I did, but it was all out of focus. I called upon God only when I personally needed Him to help me cope with my inabilities; now I began to see that my life had circulated around my own values, ideas and ego. I had misconceived the fact that Jesus suffered on the cross to save the lives of others, including me.

After the previous night's terrifying yet wonderful experience, I began the day praising God. I was inspired to eat and I did, but was over-enthusiastic. I was sick and had a tremendous pain; I lay quietly sobbing. The pain in my stomach became so great with the effort of increased eating, like a rupture at times. My skin was dry, my arms, legs and back had excessive fine hair growing and my head hair was moulting rapidly. I felt so degraded and I began to feel, 'Why bother?' Then I read in the magazine *Every day with Jesus*, 'Many people these days give up too easily. One harsh word of criticism, one lost battle in the war, and they lose heart and enthusiasm.'

After reading that, I decided that however difficult it might be I was not going to be defeated by a callous illness such as anorexia. It might be a very difficult illness to overcome but I made up my mind that I was not going to take the 'why bother?' attitude. I was going to fight it through to the end and cling on to my faith.

At visiting time, when my mother walked in, I was sitting up in bed. I was so full of my amazing experience that I hardly let her reach the bed before I said, 'Mum, I've got something to tell you,' and proceeded to describe the events of the previous night and following day. My mother was very pleased and could see that I had changed.

12 | *NEVER-ENDING NIGHT*

My life was in one hand,
I said, 'let me fall or stand,'
And with sadness did I speak
To feel so weak.

I prayed that the pain
Might soon wane,
As drifting in and out of sleep
Silent tears did I weep.

Until You entered my heart
Setting all fear apart,
And gave me the courage to fight
The never-ending night.

I hold my heart in my hand,
Before God's face I stand,
All love I have, I bring;
Unto You do I sing.

(Aged 17)

The days ticked on; my weight had both its ups and downs. Each day I benefited inasmuch as I learned about other people's difficulties. I began to see the similarities in struggling towards normal health between my illness and other illnesses. Within the same ward there were people suffering from overweight problems and cancer, and also those who had taken overdoses and were seriously ill. I got on well with one woman in particular, who had taken an overdose. She often looked at the illustrated diary that I kept, and I think the short spell in hospital faced with people struggling to live, while she had tried to take her life, gave her the will to live again. There were several patients who had had strokes and a few with lung complications, one of whom was about a year younger than me. We played chess together and sat and talked, mostly about dancing.

The difference between the other patients and me was that they came and went and I stayed. The only other person who had been there as long as I had was Winnie. She was trying to lose weight but the process was complicated by her being in a wheelchair. She would often zoom along to my bed and chat for half an hour. She mentioned a woman a couple of beds away, Mary, whom she thought I might like to meet. I ambled along to see her and almost immediately we became great friends. I benefited through her experiences as she did through mine. Her problem was that she kept on becoming anaemic and the doctors were puzzled as to where the blood was going. There were no signs of her passing blood from anywhere, yet a few days after each transfusion she became cold and pale; the blood had mysteriously disappeared.

The days continued to add up. I was slowly progressing, my head began to feel a little lighter and I could appreciate each day's happenings. I was actually becoming aware of everyday life; it was like stepping out of a cloud. My weight was creeping up but I still was not hungry, as if the gastric juices were refusing to churn, and I looked upon food with disgust. I was improving but I was still frightened and confused. The weighing scales continued to confront and accost me; I wished they would just go away. It seemed as though they ruled my life.

'Why can't you just leave my weight alone?' I asked Nurse G. in desperation.

'We can't afford to, Helena, it could have fatal effects upon your kidneys, liver or blood. I know it's difficult but you must try to help us. Why not try to take one thing at a time, eat something you wouldn't normally have as a sacrifice for someone else?'

'Okay, I'll try. But I just can't face it; I don't want anything and I feel so pressurised,' I replied.

'Don't try to face a meal, just take a little and often. But don't be put off by a meal; if you can't face it eat at least a little and then if you feel hungry later I'll always bring you something along.'

'Yes,' I replied hesitantly and not too convinced.

'Listen, you like strawberries and raspberries, don't you?'

'Yes.'

'Well, why not try a little milk on them? It won't make a lot of difference but it will just give you a few more nutrients.'

I felt a little more encouraged; Nurse G. was so understanding and gentle, with a non-pressurising attitude.

Shortly afterwards the dietician came. 'Hello, Helena, how are you feeling?'

'All right, thanks,' I replied.

'Let's have a look at the chart,' she said, glancing up at the weight graph and then down at her calculations. 'Oh dear, I think I would like the liquid build-ups increased. Without that the calories are only in the hundreds, not between two and three thousand. How do you feel about it?'

'I don't want the build-ups increased,' I admitted. I did not particularly like them.

'The more they are increased, the more your weight goes up. Perhaps the nurses could give them to you between each meal.'

I felt disheartened but agreed just for the sake of peace. Then she mentioned that my haemoglobin count was low and that she wanted me to receive more iron.

Next, one of the doctors, quite out of the blue, came over to me and said that he would like my stomach looked at after a meal. He gave no explanation as to why he wanted it to be looked at and how the doctors would do this. I was left in the dark. I knew the doctors were only trying to do their best, so it was not having my stomach looked at that scared me but the fact that the illness was such a mystery.

In many ways I longed to be happy and healthy, yet there was something preventing me from wanting to get better. As well as the sight and smell of food nauseating me terribly, I was terrified of putting on weight. It is a situation that can only be fully understood by sufferers of anorexia themselves, because it is so obscure. I am sure that most people must find it very difficult to understand why anorexics resist putting on weight; they are emaciated and quite obviously the first stage of recovery is to increase their weight. It sounds so simple, but having to force food down when even the sight of it is enough to nauseate one is not easy. Then there is the fear that whatever one eats leads to an increase in weight, and the terrifying feeling that gaining one pound, then one stone, will lead to never being able to stop putting weight on. This is complicated further by anorexics not being able to see how thin they are. Instead, when they look in the mirror they visualise a body covered in fat: not just flesh, but fat.

I felt very low-spirited, probably because of being told that the liquid build-ups had to be increased. With the amount of calories that were going into me daily I felt like a pig being fattened for carving. It was a horrible feeling, but when I tried to escape it I felt trapped. I was stuck in a maze, lost and confused, my life surrounded by paths leading to dead ends. I followed one after another desperately trying to find an escape. There was no escape; there was no end. 'Is life worth living if there's no end to my misery?' I thought to myself. 'No, it isn't.'

I thought of Mrs T., who had died of cancer that day.

She was a wonderful person; her faith so deep, her courage so strong. She fought her illness to the end despite the tremendous pain and the knowledge that she was dying.

Mrs T. and I had both found great comfort in the Wednesday ward Communions. Before breakfast the chaplain would set up a little altar in the centre. It was a beautiful and peaceful time. There was also a small chapel downstairs, which my mother and I had attended on the first Sunday but not since. One Sunday, though, Mary, the woman who kept losing blood, suggested we go to the service together. It was a lovely idea and sister allowed Mary to have breakfast by my bed before we went down. One of the nurses assisted us down the stairs as we were so weak. The service was beautiful and moved both of us greatly.

Afterwards there were no nurses to help us back and we must have looked funnier than any comedians, helping each other up the stairs in our night-clothes.

I desperately needed the strength the Communion service had given me on the following day when I was faced with a barium meal and X-ray.

At 11.30 pm on the Sunday, one of the nurses brought me a drink and pinned a notice above my bed. I twisted round to read it, half expecting it to say, 'For Sale,' but it said 'Nil after midnight.'

As usual I was woken up at 6.30 am. At breakfast-time I was quite content that I was not allowed anything to eat. The next few hours were simply anticipation as I sat and waited. One of the nurses gave me a white gown to change into, then a porter arrived and wrapped me up in a red blanket and wheeled me down to the X-ray department. I waited, quietly watching outpatients come and go. I heard my name called, 'Helena Wilkinson.' A nurse collected my notes and wheeled me into a dimly lit room filled with large metal equipment.

'Hello Helena,' the doctor said. He gave me 20 white

pills to swallow with two sips of water, a not-too-difficult feat. He then produced a carton of emulsion-like liquid with a straw. This had to be sipped at intervals, when directed, once I was on the X-ray table. The mass of equipment was most impressive and I was gently tilted back into a horizontal position, looking up at the metal monsters above me. Every now and then as I held the white liquid in the mouth the command to swallow came. A television screen lit up, and when the X-ray was switched on I saw my insides appear on the screen. This was repeated several times and then I was turned on my side. The hip bones of my emaciated body ground into the metal; my limbs turned blue with cold.

How thankful I was when the performance was finished. The porter wheeled me back to bed and handed my notes to sister. I felt terrible and just lay exhausted, huddled on my bed in my white gown and still wrapped in the red blanket. But there was to be no peace that day. In no time a woman in a white overall was beside me. I glanced at the needle in her hand.

'Not more blood,' I said.

'Yes, more blood.'

I pulled my lifeless body up the bed and placed my arm in front of her. She slid the needle in; nothing happened. She pushed it still further. I felt incredibly sick.

'Your veins are rather small and your pulse weak. Let's try the other arm.'

Reluctantly I gave her the other arm. In slid the needle; I felt myself drifting off and groaned. She laid me down as I went out. Unbelievably, when I came round she said, 'Right love, we'll give it one more try.'

I felt drained and I lay motionless for the rest of that day. I cannot remember eating anything and the only time I was moved was for weighing, still lying wrapped up in the red blanket.

In the afternoon the physician came and told me that the X-ray had shown no blockage, but my stomach had shrunk severely and needed to be stretched. I suppose it was quite a relief, but at that moment I could not have cared what news he brought. He admitted that they were not having great success with me, and said that he was calling in the aid of a child psychiatrist.

I do not remember anything else about that day except that when my mother came to visit me after school I was still lying huddled on my bed in the X-ray gown. She brought with her a shaft of sunlight. After she had helped me back into my night-clothes we prayed together, as we did every night of my stay in hospital. They were simple, straightforward prayers: clasping my hands in hers in a sign of unity of purpose and caring, we would pray for the doctors and nurses, the other patients, sometimes specifically by name, and lastly for me. This night in particular these prayers gave me back my strength, my peace and the determination not to let my faith slide.

It was also at this stage in my life I came to know a man from the Salvation Army, who I know had much to do with me getting better. He had bright eyes and was a bouncy little fellow; apart from visiting me in hospital, he kept sending me very talkative letters to try to cheer me up. He would begin by saying, 'Hello Cheerie Cherub!' Though he had very little money he frequently enclosed a fifty-pence piece for me to buy sweets! Many of his letters contained jokes in an attempt to brighten my world. But more important was his strong faith and belief that God could heal me from anorexia. He woke at 4.30 am each morning and would lie flat on the floor in his little home to pray for me and many others. He was a remarkable man and I will always be grateful for his faithfulness.

13 | *HIDDEN TEARS*

As for me
I dream of how
Life used to be;
The people for whom
I cared,
For the memories
I shared.

Hidden tears
Behind my eyes
Reveal the fears
Which my mind
Now knows;
Such pain my body
Shows.

But every day
I quietly sit
And pray
For others' pain
I see,
Thanking God for the good
In me.

(Aged 19)

One day one of the staff nurses helped me along to a little room outside the ward to see two of the team of child psychiatrists who had been called in. The strangest thing was shaking hands with two men whilst dressed in my night-clothes! I perched on the edge of the chair, whilst one of the doctors told me exactly what anorexia is and the effects it can have upon you. Then they began to ask questions about my past history. They seemed very nice people, and to my surprise I soon began to feel at ease. They appeared very concerned that after a long spell in hospital I had not really shown any sign of improvement. One of them asked to see my arms; I pulled up my sleeve in response.

'Look, what d'you think?' he said to the other man.

'Yes, it's quite bad,' he replied.

'Can you lean forward a minute, love, so that we can look at the top of your back.'

I leant forward; he pulled my dressing-gown away from my neck.

'Yes,' he sighed, 'It's pretty serious.'

They explained that the lanugo (fine hair) that appeared especially on the arms, and in extreme cases down the back and around the face, was one of the features of anorexia. They asked if I had it on my legs, especially my thighs; I admitted I had and felt degraded by it.

'We're going to put you on complete bed rest; that means you can't get up for anything at all.'

That would not make a vast amount of difference, just that there would be no more physiotherapy and I would depend on my bell a lot more.

'We'll also try increasing the Largactil to 75 mg three times a day.'

'Sounds like I am back at square one,' I thought to myself.

We're sending someone along to talk to you once a week. She's a child psychiatrist, and she'll see you and your parents together first and then you by yourself.'

I was not very enthusiastic about the idea, but went along with it.

'I'll be going along to talk to your parents within the next few days and we'll see how things go from there.'

I said goodbye and found my own way back to the ward.

Back in the ward I could take stock of how bed rest would affect me. To lose the physiotherapy seemed partly good and partly bad. Early on, the doctor had wanted me to have regular gentle exercise and so had asked my mother to take me swimming. A good friend who was the headmistress of a local school allowed us to use the swimming pool after the girls had finished. It was lovely to get out of hospital, but I was so weak I had almost to learn to swim again.

For some strange reason the doctors then stopped this happy outing and changed me to hospital physiotherapy, which was less pleasant. Whether they thought this would help to strengthen my muscles more quickly, I do not know, but I exchanged my contact with the outside world for a burgundy tracksuit and the dreariness of the hospital gymnasium. There was a hard board to lie on, straps on my legs and bean-bags, which increased in weight each day, on my ankles. Every day, with increasing weakness, after weight-loss and extra exercise I felt more and more exhausted. I was therefore not sorry to say goodbye to physiotherapy for the moment.

Unfortunately, I was not the only person who had become worse. My friend Mary suddenly haemorrhaged badly and was rushed to another ward. I thought about her a lot. She was a splendid example of courage. We kept in touch through my mother or the newspaper boy. One morning I received a letter from her that meant a tremendous amount to me.

Dear Helena,
I've been thinking of you quite a lot since I left the ward

111

on Friday. The little text did help, and it came along with another little miracle which I'll have to tell you or your mother about. I'm not like you, dear, I don't express myself very well on paper.

Like me I hear that you're confined to your bed, so I only hope it's having a good effect on you, dear; it is on me. I am still too sore to want to move around much, but now that my drip is off my arm and the tubes out of my nose I'm feeling better all the time.

Sunday morning at Communion time I thought about our going down together the Sunday before. I'm so glad we made it; I was able to go through it all in my head. Well, love, I'm having breakfast this morning, my first food since last Thursday so I'm ready for it, and it's just going on the rounds. I want Ivor the paper boy to be postman for me so it will have to be cheerio for now.

Don't give up your fighting spirit, Helena. I know with the help of Jesus you will beat this illness. I can see your name in print, for I'm sure that one day you will be famous. This spell in hospital also has its purpose of making you aware of your own capabilities, and it's an experience that God must want you to have. Unpleasant though it may be now, I'm sure that soon it will be all behind you. So God bless you, dear, I shall never forget the pleasure of knowing you. I hope to get up to see you all in 'Adelaide' soon.

Love Mary.

The miracle that she mentioned in her letter was that she had received the laying on of hands by a pastor, and the blood that she had been given had *not* disappeared. If everything was well after several days then she could go home. It was; the blood stayed and no further transfusion was needed – it was incredible. I had not been happier in weeks than when I heard that she could definitely go home in a few days' time. It certainly was a miracle.

I just kept praying to God that He would help me to overcome this illness and lose my profound fear, but it was more than I could cope with; I became depressed and began to cry. I was lost in a terrifying world; fear just ran through my blood, and my body became flushed as the tears trickled down my drab face.

'Don't worry.'

I peered up through my tear-stricken eyes and saw Nurse G. sympathetically looking down at me. She drew the curtains round my bed and sat down.

'You don't want all those people watching, do you?'

'No,' I mumbled, trying to hold back the tears.

'Have a cry if you want, Helena. You've had to put up with a lot recently, and now you can't move from your bed for anything. I think that's really unfair.'

'So do I. It's really degrading having to use a bed-pan and not being able to do anything without a nurse there. I can't bear it any longer.'

I felt the lump in my throat get bigger, I swallowed hard and bit my lip.

'Have lots of milky drinks.'

The thought repelled me; tears surged forward. 'I hate milk,' I said sharply.

'Oh dear! You were drinking it quite a lot at one time and your weight was going up. Now it's below six stone again.'

'I can't drink milk any more,' I said.

'I know it's difficult, Helena, but people have won through, and you must try. So many people don't understand just what a fight it is, but you believe in God, don't you?'

'Yes, that's the only thing that's stopped me from giving up,' I replied.

'Well, don't give up, please.'

We sat chatting for a while; then she left me. She had given me the reassurance that I so desperately needed at that moment. I knew that I must not give up as I looked at two girls in nearby beds who had taken overdoses; they had tried to take their own lives, because they were unable to face the future. If I gave up now, I would be doing exactly the same: I would be taking an easy way out of facing my problems. As hard as it seemed, I now wanted to face the future, and yet before Nurse G. had spoken to me, I had wished that I did not exist. The endless depressions and the grip of the illness were mental torture, and the simplest way to put an end to it was an end to life. I knew I could not do this; I had to persevere.

14 | CARRYING MY LOAD

> *When the hills in life*
> *Are hard to climb,*
> *The paths are*
> *Dusty and steep,*
> *When walking takes*
> *Too long in time*
> *And I feel that*
> *I could weep,*
> *That's when I learn*
> *To run the race,*
> *Towards the One who*
> *I know will care.*
> *Through the radiance*
> *In His face*
> *I know I'm always*
> *Welcome there.*

(Aged 16)

During one of the visiting times when my mother was with me, the child psychiatrist came. I was very weak and did not feel like talking; however, I complied. Her questions were very personal and I felt incredibly awkward when she asked my mother about her marriage in front of me. Unfortunately she just was not the right person to help me; she brought back painful memories. I know that is what psychiatry is concerned with, but she made no attempt to heal them.

Each time I saw her she mentioned that she wanted me to go to the hospital where she worked, but first I would have to reach 6 stone 7 pounds. She said there would be other young people with similar and different problems; there would be a lot of activity going on; there would also be medical staff keeping an eye on my condition. At one point she almost convinced me that it would be a good idea, that I would have friends of my own age, I would not be stuck in a hospital bed all day and I would benefit by hearing other people's problems as well as discussing my own.

Then I realised I would be in an institution, a hospital environment – a psychiatric hospital at that – for weeks, possibly months, surrounded only by young people, some with problems a lot worse than mine. I would doubtless go from better to worse. There would be little hope for the future, and my career prospects would be ruined. Valuable years of my life would be lost by simply dwelling on my illness and being bound by the past – what a ghastly thought! I decided I would be better off where I was, even if I could not move around for the time being.

I had been confined to bed for several weeks when one day there was a break in the monotony. In the morning we had the ward service, which was an inspiration for the rest of the day for several of us. Then I had two surprise visitors, a sister from a nearby convent school who was very kind, and Helen, the girl who had been in the next bed several weeks back. It was great to see her again and hear all her news. She brought me some beautiful sweet peas from her garden which brightened my corner up. It had been a long time since we had seen one another and we chatted for quite some time until my father came in. I felt quite exhausted after having three visitors in succession.

In the afternoon I heard some of the student nurses talking about a fire practice. Then one said to me, 'You're on complete bed rest aren't you?'

'Yes. What's going on?' I replied.

'Oh, we're going to have a fire practice throughout the hospital. Those on complete bed rest are either left in bed or carried in a blanket or stretcher, and other patients are assisted down the fire escapes. It's just so that we can carry out the practical procedures,' she explained.

'What will happen to me, then?' I asked.

'I don't know. Sister will tell you.'

I was all for drama. It looked like a bit of fun as I watched the nurses practise carrying each other in blankets as a stretcher. Then the sister came over.

'Hello, Helena. You don't want to miss out on the fun, do you?'

'No!' I replied in an enthusiastic voice.

'Well, I'll let one of the student nurses accompany you to the edge of the fire escape.'

I was so pleased I could join in the fun and have the opportunity to get out of bed. A first-year student nurse came along and helped me up to the fire escape; my legs felt as though they had seized up and were very weak. I shuffled along to the door. As I approached it, fresh air whirled around my head, sweet-smelling summer air, birds singing and the sun warm and shining brightly. It brought an immediate feeling of joy and beauty to my heart. I took a deep breath and sighed heavily. Sister had told me to go only as far as the door, but the nurse proceeded to take me down the stairs out into the open. I presumed sister had changed her mind so I made every effort to go. Besides, the fresh air was so welcoming that I was prepared to push myself, but it was a struggle to get back up to the top again; I was exhausted.

The following day was unfortunately rather more than just an anti-climax. I can only presume it happened because of the previous day's activities. I was woken up at 6.00 am shortly after which the staff nurse came to take my blood pressure. They always took two readings, one lying, the other standing. I did not know a lot about blood pressure except that mine was well below normal. The nurse wound the strip around my arm and began to pump.

'We don't seem to be doing too well today, I can't get a reading.' She paused for a while. 'Ah yes, here we are.'

She scribbled down some figures and asked me to stand up. I promptly pushed the bedclothes aside and stood by the bed. She wound the strip around my arm and once more began to pump. I suddenly felt incredibly sick and shuffled back a few paces to prop my body up against the bed to give me the extra security. The strip around my arm deflated.

'I don't seem to be able to get a reading this time either,' she said in a rather concerned voice.

'Please don't try again, just let me lie down,' I thought to myself.

'I'll try again,' she said.

Only this time she pumped it up a little tighter. I felt the blood rush from my head; the warm liquid flowed down my body and once more I felt incredibly sick, as though my head was clamped between metal tongs.

'Help. I'm going,' I mumbled.

The nurse rang my bell and called for assistance. Immediately another nurse arrived. They lifted me on to the bed, drew the curtains round and began to wind the handle at the end to raise the bottom of my bed. The last thing I remember before I went out was, 'Call the night sister quick.'

When I came round it was amazingly peaceful; the curtains were still drawn around my bed, but the sun was streaming in through the window. My feet were still much higher than my head; it was a strange sensation. I do not know what happened whilst I was unconscious or how long I had been that way; all I could remember was the bustle that took place beforehand. I lay in that position for quite some time before I asked one of the nurses if I could be lowered. The blood had re-entered my head but I felt incredibly weak and drained of all energy. The staff nurse came along and lowered my bed. I just lay there, mesmerised, until my mother came at visiting time. I think the news was rather a shock to her, but she was very good with her courage and support, as were many people. I do not think anything could have replaced those small touches of friendship that brought reassurance.

After my parents had gone in the evening, I had an extreme wave of depression; every minute seemed an hour long and I wished I could drop off to sleep and wake up completely better, as though the entire illness had been a bad dream. At times I even believed I was having a bad dream and that I would soon wake up and forget it all, once again enjoying myself in everyday activities. 'Everyday activities,' I thought to myself, 'they're non-existent at the moment and will probably remain that way for a long time.' All the memories of the sports I participated in at school came flooding back, the tremendous sensation of one's body flying through the air after a neck spring, the mystique of tap dancing; I could not bear to think of these any more, my eyes filled with tears. It was a vicious circle, too vicious, and I was just going round and round it, being torn to shreds.

The night staff had just come on duty and were going round each bed, sliding the headrest into the sleeping position and shaking up the pillows. I saw one of the auxiliaries coming in my direction: she was ever such a sweet woman, so gentle and caring. I closed my tear-stained eyes in haste.

'Hello, poppet,' she said in her usual cheery voice.

I did not reply. I thought it better not to, for I knew that if I were to open my mouth I would burst into tears.

'You're not asleep are you?'

I slowly revealed my red eyes. 'No,' I replied, almost choking as the tears surged forward.

'Oh, my little poppet, don't cry.' She pushed my hair away from my forehead and wiped the tears away from my cheeks. 'What's wrong?' she asked with great concern.

'I don't know,' I whispered.

'Oh poppet,' she said once more, still softly stroking my face.

She put my headrest down and helped me to sit up whilst she puffed my pillows, then took such care over making sure I was comfortable and tucking me in. The tears began to dry up. I felt a lot better for that cry; her gentle motherly approach had calmed my heart and soothed me. She pushed my hair away from my face once more and bent down to kiss me goodnight.

'Sleep well,' she whispered, and moved on to the next bed.

I felt so peaceful, I just closed my eyes and fell asleep.

I woke up to a fantastic surprise, to hear from the physician that I could go home in just over a week's time. I could hardly believe my ears; it was marvellous news. Naturally, there had to be an 'if' to follow – if I could maintain my weight. I did not have to put on more weight, just maintain my present weight. I had not reached my target weight, but the summer holidays were coming up and with much persuasion the doctors decided to let me home on a trial basis as my mother would be there during the day. My mother had pointed out to them that I had actually got *worse* in hospital; and she wanted to help me at home and was willing to take the responsibility.

How those days till the end of my being in hospital dragged on! It was like the last few feet of climbing Mount Everest; each day seemed longer and longer, and I certainly was not without my difficulties, either. I wondered when it would all end, but I realised that it was important at this stage to look back and compare it with the earlier times, recognising the trials I had been through and had managed to overcome.

At the start of the following week the doctors came round and confirmed that I could go home on Friday. I really felt they meant it this time. My weight had not fallen for several days and they were obviously pleased that I had managed to maintain it; they recognised stability in my illness. For once the sun was shining in my life, and I could not wait to tell my parents the news that my coming home was definite. During visiting hours we sat and talked about the things we would do together when I had left hospital.

I was, however, a little worried about going home and how I would cope, as I knew that I was nowhere near cured of anorexia. Whether I was in hospital or at home, I still faced the same problem – that I was anorexic. Although I knew that at home I would have the support of my parents, I was also aware that I would no longer have the security that I was used to in hospital. As well as facing the difficulties over eating, I would have to cope with the pressures from a hostile world. Even so, I was looking forward to leaving hospital and being in a more natural environment. I had seen so many people come and go, I could not believe that at last I was the one going.

The night before I was due to leave I just could not sleep. My toes kept on twitching with excitement and my mind was bubbling away. I was woken up at 6.00 am.

'Who's going home today then?'

It was the voice of the same auxiliary nurse who had been so kind the evening that I was feeling depressed. I turned over, opened my eyes and smiled.

'I can't believe it,' I said.

The morning was the longest I had ever experienced – anticipation, I suppose. After breakfast the paper boy came on the rounds with his trolley. I always knew it was him with his outbursts of whistles, song and corny jokes. He was enough to give you inspiration on a dreary morning! He had not had a lot of custom from me but he always passed a joke in my direction. When Helen had been in the next bed, he would start singing or chatting about the two terrible Helens – double trouble!

I had my curtain still drawn round me but I could hear

his cheery voice and squeaking wheels coming in my direction. I wanted to say goodbye to him, but there was no hope. I was shut in. I could see the outline of the trolley outside my curtains, then I heard, 'First there was double trouble, then trouble, and now there'll be no trouble!'

I knew he was referring to the fact that I was going today. 'That's right,' I added.

'Bye then, Helen number two,' he said in a raised humorous voice.

'Bye,' I replied.

The medicine trolley came round. I thought perhaps I would be relieved of any drugs seeing that I was going home, but obviously that was just wishful thinking. The sun streamed in through the window and beat on my back. I lay and imagined myself on a warm, sandy beach, surrounded by tropical plants, the gentle swishing of the waves lulling me to sleep – then Concorde flew over and ruined my fantasy world. After lunch I sat and waited patiently.

'Hello. I've come to check your belongings.'

One of the student nurses handed me a black plastic bag, helped me to put everything that I had with me into it, then drew the curtains round and told me to get dressed. I changed into the towelling tracksuit which I had used for physiotherapy and sat on the edge of my bed. Then I heard the scales being pushed in my direction.

'You don't want to weigh me, do you?' I asked sister with foreboding.

'Afraid so,' she replied with a smile.

'Can I sit on the scales like this or do I have to change into the usual clothes?'

'You'll have to change, I'm afraid, love, otherwise it will give an incorrect reading.'

So once again I changed, only to have to re-dress afterwards. I watched expectantly while she marked my new weight on the graph. 'Help!' I gasped to myself, 'I've gone down, that means I won't be going home today.' Luckily, however, it did not affect my being able to leave. Minor changes in weight can occur due to water balance.

Shortly afterwards my mother arrived. I saw her talking to sister; she was presenting the basket of fruit which she had bought as a thank you to all the nurses.

I said all my goodbyes to the other patients that I knew and then to the nurses. The porter wheeled me to the nurses' station and down towards the door of the ward.

'Don't come back, will you, Helena?' Sister called after me with a smile.

'I'll come to see you, but not stay.'

So off I went, still very much underweight and still with a long road to recovery. My muscles had wasted so much that while I had walked into hospital I left in a wheelchair, with very little energy or ability to sustain walking for any length of time.

15 | *PRETENCE*

Pretend you're happy when you're blue
It isn't very hard to do,
Close your eyes and you'll be there
To find a world that'll really care.

The blazing earth will no longer burn
And fear never return,
The darkening shadow shall flee
Setting your heart free.

The glimmering landscape comes into sight
But to keep the sun is no longer a fight,
There is no rugged path in life
Along which you struggle and strive.

No more is there an ocean bare,
Love and happiness ride there,
And people stand with their arms wide
Warmly to welcome you inside.

(Aged 17)

The birds' songs were melodious, the smell of the flowers sweet, the sky blue and the sun felt warm on my face as I was wheeled from the overpowering smell of medication in the hospital out into the fresh air. I stood up and took a deep breath, inhaling the pureness of the air. How exhilarated I felt to face the summer in all its glory. There certainly was no melancholy in that short-lived moment of my life! The strangest thing was having left the memories of spring behind when I was taken into hospital, and stepping out to see the summer in its prime, as though the past three months had been totally non-existent.

As I climbed into the car ready to be taken home, I could feel the radiance from my mother's face. It must have been a wonderful time for her too, after having driven away from her frequent visits with a lonely, empty feeling. This time that empty space was filled and she was taking me home for good. However kind everyone had been and however much I had become a part of Adelaide Ward, it was a relief to be leaving it behind. We turned into a wide road, each side lined by shady trees, and headed for the town centre. The world seemed so busy, as though it had been speeded up, cars zooming past and people dashing from shop to shop. It was exhausting to watch.

It was mid-afternoon by the time we arrived home. Immediately I was greeted by my cat who rapturously rubbed against my legs, purring with content. I felt as though I was in another world; it was strange to see so much activity and life. I felt a new appreciation and sensitivity towards the world; everything was so beautiful – the luscious green trees, the multi-coloured flowers, the smell of new-mown grass and the way in which the sun blazed from a brilliant blue sky. There was so much colour and beauty all around. It was such a lovely day that it seemed a shame not to be out in the open and enjoying it, so after I had had a drink my mother put a sunlounger in the garden and I sat down on it, half shaded by the crab-apple tree.

No sooner had I sat down than the doorbell went. My mother answered it, and came over to me carrying a beautiful bouquet of flowers; they were from my Salvation Army friend, whom I nicknamed 'Bright Eyes', because his eyes sparkled and he added brightness to my life.

Then a neighbour came over with some sweet peas from her garden, and another came round with a welcome home card and some notelets.

I had only been sitting outside for about fifteen minutes when my face began to itch furiously, and then the irritation spread to my legs and arms. It became so intense that I was forced to retreat inside. The same thing happened the following day. I was sitting in the shade, but after no more than about ten minutes my skin began to itch and then burn terribly; I could not bear to be outside any longer. I did not understand why this was happening as I had never been allergic to the sun before. I discovered that I was suffering from some of the many side-effects of the drug, Largactil, I had been put on in hospital. I had received no warning about potential side-effects, which as well as sensitivity to sun included lowering blood pressure when my blood pressure was already low and affecting eyesight when I was already partially-sighted. Also, I was not taken off Largactil or sleeping tablets slowly; despite receiving high dosages in hospital, all medication was stopped the day I left!

For the first few weeks after leaving hospital I slept downstairs, as I was still very weak. My muscles had wasted away, having not had any exercise or even physiotherapy for a couple of months. This meant that day-to-day activities, including walking, were both tiring and painful. I found that I was waking up very early in the morning and by mid-afternoon was extremely tired, so I usually slept for a couple of hours after lunch. To begin with I was still eating very little indeed and my weight, rather than increasing, fell to barely 6 stone again. My mother feared that I would lose even more and said that whatever happened I must try to keep my weight above 6 stone. I found eating very difficult. It was a battle of will, but was helped by my mother taking me out to pub lunches. We nearly always had mixed salads and meat as I found that raw foods, unlike cooked foods, did not nauseate me and the variety of salads and the good presentation made the meal far more appetising.

My parents were very supportive during this time. They were aware of both my physical pain and my mental turmoil, and did all that they could to help me. Besides my mother taking me out to pub lunches, we would visit new places, spend the day in scenic areas and go for picnics by the river. My sister and I were getting on a lot better, and when she came home at weekends we would quite often do things together as a family. It was lovely to feel united as a family and to be able to talk to Ruth about ordinary, everyday things without feelings of bitterness and jealousy between us. When I was in hospital she was supportive in sending me lots of get-well cards and we began to see each other more as individuals rather than enemies.

As good as my family were to me, I could not help feeling disheartened over the life that I was leading. I watched other girls of 16 and 17 start new jobs, drive around on mopeds and socialise in the evenings. They led happy, independent lives – and there was I, sitting at home struggling to regain normal health, watching my young life, supposedly the happiest days of my life, slip away before my very eyes. Compared with the average teenager I was living in a solitary, unhappy world.

As the weeks went past, the feeling of having to 'make it to the top' pressed upon me heavily. I sat back and thought about my solitary world and the unrealistic life that I was leading. My life benefited no one, and particularly not mine. Ever since I had left hospital I had wasted valuable time and achieved nothing worthwhile. I thought to myself, 'I should be getting on with living, not sitting around waiting.' I am the sort of person who has to be busy doing something to feel that I am worthwhile. For me life has to have meaning and an objective. If I do not have a sense of achievement, as I did not at that time, then life is a waste of time. I became restless and knew that I

127

had to find something to do: I succeeded in getting a part-time job as a breakfast waitress. The hotel was only two minutes' walk from my house, and the work involved just a couple of hours early in the morning. The job was ideal: it gave me the independence and sense of achievement I needed without being too tiring.

I was beginning to organise my life and feel in command again. I had acquired a keen interest in cooking and spent a lot of time preparing foods that I would not allow myself to eat, such as cakes, taking great care and precision over the decoration. I enjoyed making and decorating cakes, but considered them to be a piece of artwork, to be viewed by all and eaten by anyone except myself! I had not put on much weight, but was happy like that; I neither felt fat nor thin and was managing to eat just enough to keep me going. I was enjoying some foods although I had no appetite or, should I say, hunger.

I think it is important to know the difference between appetite and hunger. I consider appetite to be something that the mind desires, and hunger to be something that the stomach desires. When someone has an appetite then they fancy food because it is to their liking; if on the other hand someone has no appetite then they feel nauseated by food. When someone is hungry then their bodies crave food because their gastric juices are churning and their glycogen supplies are in need of replenishment; if someone is not hungry then they have no hunger pains.

I was thankful that the child psychiatrist had not managed to admit me into the psychiatric hospital as she had wanted to. I would still have been in hospital, surrounded by sick and emotionally troubled, or even mentally disturbed, people. My whole life would have been centred around my weight, diet and emotional conflicts. It would have been months before I could have left. The thought of still being in hospital was unbearable. At least being at home I could get on with living, and not have to worry about reaching a target weight. Yet at times

I wished that I was in hospital, receiving medical help and support from outside the family, or with someone trying to help me to understand why I felt the way I did. Really I did not know what I wanted; I was confused.

A month after I had started my part-time job I decided that I needed to think about my future career. I could not bear the thought of working for only two hours a day and not training for a career. I could not bear the thought of returning to my old school and my idea of taking spanish, food and nutrition, and art A levels at a nearby convent school followed by a BA in graphic design, had fallen through; the thought of any school was too much. So, I had to think again. Besides art, I had been keen on food and nutrition whilst studying for my O levels. My thoughts about taking a catering course were confirmed when I received a telephone call from my headmistress. I had been graded on two O levels which I should have taken and she had the results:

'I've got your two latest O level results, Helena. Are you ready?'

'Yes,' I replied with anticipation and excitement.

'History first: B for Betty, then Food and Nutrition: A for Aunty. Have you got that? Aunty Betty!'

I was really pleased and straightaway I started to look through college prospectuses for suitable courses. I decided to apply for the general catering course which would give me City and Guilds qualifications. My application was seven months too late, but nevertheless I was called up for an interview.

The day that the interview was taking place, I had an appointment to see the consultant physician at the hospital. He was very pleased with the progress I had made. I had managed to put on some weight, and at 6 stone 6 pounds I was only one pound under the weight he had set for me to reach before leaving hospital. He was pleased that I was going along for an interview at the technical college, wished me good luck, and made another appointment for me to see him. As I went from the hospital to the college I thought one thing: 'Thank goodness I am taking a step towards my career, not a hospital bed!'

When I arrived at the college, I had a very informal interview with the head of the Department of Food, Health and Fashion. He advised me to take an Ordinary National Diploma in Hotel and Catering Operations and offered me a place on the course to commence in two weeks. I owe many thanks to the head of the department for accepting me whilst I was still very ill and could have been a liability.

I really had an incentive to get better. I knew that if I wanted to get the diploma then I had to keep well enough to carry out the two years' work. I could not let myself, my family or the college down by having to go back into hospital. I felt exhilarated that I had done something positive and that the prospects for the future were looking quite good. I did not have much time to worry about whether I would cope with life at college because there was such a lot to distract my attention. There was my equipment and clothing to buy, visits to the Local Education Authority and many other things.

The day before the enrolment I became very apprehensive. I was not sure how easy it would be to make friends and what people would think of my appearance. I wondered how I would be able to stand up to the day-to-day activities: walking, climbing the never-ending stairs and writing at fast speed. I worried about how I would cope with lunchtimes: young people wolfing down packets of crisps, cans of coke and bars of chocolate. At some point I would no doubt be compelled to join in with these crazy habits, but the thought was daunting.

The enrolment day came and I was amazed by the relaxed atmosphere of the college, the freedom and the respect which the tutors had for their students as individuals. They were always making jokes which enabled us as students to feel more on a level with the tutors. We were not constantly spoken down to; we were treated like adults. It was quite different from what I had been used to at my convent school and I knew that if I tried hard I could enjoy myself. By the end of the first day my conviction that I was going to be happy had grown. I had really enjoyed the lectures and I had made friends with one of the girls on the course. We remained friends for the two years. I was, however, extremely tired adjusting to a new routine. Going to lectures and doing some written work in the evening was as much as I could manage for the whole of the first term. All my energy was directed towards my work and I very rarely socialised. I was happy putting all my time into the course, deriving far more satisfaction from being conscientious than from socialising with people my own age. I could not laugh like other people; it was too much effort. I thought that other people would think me strange because of my appearance and apparent solemnity, and I was hypersensitive to criticism.

As the weeks progressed and I became accustomed to college life and the various subjects which the course involved, I began to feel more secure as a person, but even so I was not without my difficulties and there was one time in particular when I felt like giving up the course. Physically it was too much effort. I could not join in with the gaiety of the other students; I felt distant and alone. I lived in fear of being a failure and of criticism over my work, appearance and eating habits. I dreaded the day when we would have a test and I would not be able to read the questions on the board; the time when I would not be able to stand up to a day's work in the kitchen and I would collapse. I had been living in a world of pretence, dreaming of being on a beautiful island, covered by brilliant white sand and sparkling sea; miles of empty space to run and feel free. Then I would be forced to return to reality. When I saw the life that I was leading my dreams faded. My island of paradise changed into dark woods in which I was trapped and had no room to breathe.

Despite the knowledge that there was something wrong, the tutors did not treat me any differently from the other students, which gave me the determination to carry on as if all were well. I felt that they respected me as an individual and that they had confidence in my work and in me, even if I did not. This was particularly evident with the food science tutor, to whom I owe so much.

One of the hardest things to cope with was the production kitchen. As well as needing the energy to be on my feet for half the day and cook for large numbers, I had to cope with the vast quantity of food, the smell whirling around me. I remember the first time that I was cooking for the training restaurant; I was meat chef. Ten pounds of beef was slapped in front of me. I stuck the knife in to cut it up: blood and meat juice oozed out, the odour wafted up; there was a layer of horrible fat, and I was overcome by a profound feeling of nausea. As I cut through the mound of meat, my arm ached. I felt that I would never last out until the end of the morning – but I did! As I was leaving the room at the end of the lesson, the tutor grabbed my arm, 'You need to put some weight on,' she told me. I knew that only too well, but could not do anything about it.

She was well aware that besides lacking physical strength, I lacked self-confidence, but also knew that if I wanted to go into catering then I had to overcome both of these. There was nothing that she could do to help me overcome my physical weakness other than to warn me that I could never cope unless I put on weight, but she could help me to gain confidence. Her way of doing this was to push me to the extreme and face me with tasks that I did not believe I could carry out, thereby proving to myself that I was as capable as anyone else. At the time it did not seem to be the kindest thing to do, but it certainly made me fight and hardened me, as well as giving me the determination to succeed.

At the end of my first term at college I had another appointment with the consultant physician at the hospital. I walked rather nervously into Outpatients. I knew that I had not put on any weight and I feared what he would do. I sat down until the sister came over to me.

'Let's check your weight, Helena,' she said.

My stomach turned over as I heard the squeak of the scales being wheeled towards me. Slowly, I sat down; she checked the reading and scribbled down some figures. Then the consultant called me into his room. He looked at the notes and piece of paper which the sister had handed to him. His eyes stared straight through me, and with the house doctor also present, looking sternly at me, I felt extremely uncomfortable. Seeing the two of them standing there suddenly brought back all the memories of hospital. I remembered how I dreaded the doctor's rounds on the ward: the horrid feelings of lying in bed surrounded by white coats and staring faces, firing questions. I felt sick with fear. The feeling gradually died away as the consultant asked me how I felt and what I was doing. He was pleased that I had managed to maintain my weight and that I had been accepted at college. He decided that I was better off away from doctors and hospitals and that there was no need for me to make another appointment with him, unless at any stage my parents or I were worried. It certainly was a good start to the Christmas holidays; I was free, no longer tied to a hospital!

The following term I had something wonderful to look forward to, which helped me to get through the term with few worries. I was going to Bermuda to stay with my cousin Kathie during the Easter holidays. Ever since I had written to Kathie in desperation at boarding school I had longed to stay with her but never had the courage to ask. Not only was going to Bermuda something to look forward to and an incentive to keep well, but it was a topic to talk about in the Spoken English lecture! I used to dread Spoken English as, amongst other things, we would be put on the spot and expected to stand up and speak on a subject in front of the rest of the class. I could not see what this had to do with catering!

The term began with me catching some kind of bug. (Colds and flu were something that I had very rarely had since getting anorexia). It was not bad enough to take time off college, but left me feeling tired, dizzy and heavy-headed.

I was one of the students from the catering department taking part in the Bournemouth Food and Wine Exhibition, an exhibition and competition open to students and professional caterers. I had decided to enter the fruit cake class, and a lot of time and effort was spent on the preparation for the exhibition. Besides being very keen on the practical cookery, I took a special interest in hygiene and microbiology and food science, which included nutrition. I found them fascinating. I had never been any good at science at school, but at college I was achieving top grades. The way the subjects were taught and the manner in which we were treated as students made me want to learn and do well. I think also the fact that I was trapped in anorexia caused me to be so fascinated by anything to do with food that I would spend hours studying when other students were off socialising.

Whilst I was managing to maintain my weight (even if still at least two stone below average) I was becoming more obsessive. I weighed myself twice a day to see whether I had put on even one pound. I was not particularly trying to lose weight but I did have a growing phobia of weight gain. I was terrified that if I put on one pound it would lead to another and another, and before I knew it I would reach 7 stone. When I stood on the scales and they read 6 stone 9 pounds, I panicked; I was only 5 pounds less than the dreaded 7 stone mark.

I then looked in the mirror and the figure that stared back at me, rather than the scrawny being which others saw, was fat and ugly. This phenomenon of the mirror-image was not peculiar to me but a common factor in anorexia. You actually see a distorted picture of your body. Seeing my body looking fat and lumpy at 6 stone 9 pounds reinforced my terror at the thought of reaching 7 stone, let alone the normal 8 stone 7 pounds or 9 stone, the usual weight for women of my age and height.

My eating habits were as bizarre as my conception of weight. When I first went to college I used to go into the refectory for lunch, which usually consisted of a bowl of soup or salad; very occasionally, if I was feeling enter-prising, I would have chicken pie, carefully putting aside the pastry, of course! Later I started to take sandwiches to college. The thought of two slices of bread, spread with fat and filled with protein, was too much. I either ate the meat and disposed of the bread or else disposed of the lot in the nearest bin. I carried out this practice for nearly two years before my parents found out. I was so cunning and deceitful over hiding food that I do not think any of my college friends had a clue what was going on. In the evening I always ate with my family because I felt I had no choice, but I was very fussy over what I ate. I enjoyed planning and cooking meals, but always gave myself a very small helping; then afterwards I would go and pick at the leftovers or at food in the fridge. Where possible I avoided eating meals and food in general.

Gradually, I began to put on some weight. I felt terrible. I was depressed and full of self-loathing at my lack of control. I could not bring myself to eat full meals, but instead when no one was around I picked at food in a way that felt uncontrollable. At college we would make fresh bread rolls for the restaurant, and many of the students ate them as they came out of the oven. The smell of fresh white rolls suddenly became appealing and as I broke the crisp crust of one open the warm dough became irresistible. I pulled the doughy middle out and ate it – the texture and taste were wonderful. I realised that I loved such food but that for several years now I hadn't allowed myself to eat it in fear of what would happen to me. Half deceiving myself that I was not eating much, I would never have a whole roll but would pull out the dough from roll after roll and throw away the crust. As the weeks went by so my weight gradually crept up.

The extra pounds that I had gained made me feel as if there was something inside that did not belong to me. For so long my underweight body had expressed how fragile and vulnerable I felt as a person. Now it seemed I was getting bigger and bigger and people would expect more of me. I had reached 7 stone. Two of the girls on my course commented that I had put on weight and how much better I looked. Contrary to what one would expect, their comment made me feel even worse. The thought that other people could notice a change must mean that I had put on a lot of weight. 'I must look terrible, I must be fat,' I thought. The fact was that I could not accept that I looked different. Then, during the last week of term, I caught another flu bug. I had four days off college, during which time I lost a couple of pounds; my weight was now 6 stone 12 pounds.

16 | *THE ONE WHO LOVES ME*

I love to see
The birds flee
To their nesty bed
To have a rest;
Then when night is done,
One by one
They rouse the crowd
By singing out loud.

Strongest is the Magpie
With his screeching cry,
The voice of the Swallow
Echoes hollow,
And the song of the Tit
Is full of wit,
But the Kiskadee
Is the one who loves me.

(Aged 17)

The day after I broke up for the Easter holidays, I flew to Bermuda. My cousin Kathie was waiting at the airport to meet me. We had not seen each other for six years and I feared that she might not recognise me, but she did. Also there to greet me were the Canon of Bermuda Cathedral, Peter, and his wife Joy. Kathie had been staying with them since she had had to leave her apartment. As we drove to the city of Hamilton, where they lived, I looked out of the window at the brilliant turquoise sea, the multi-coloured houses with their white roofs and the cascades of brightly coloured flowers. The birds sang melodiously, songs which were music to my ears: one sang out repetitively, 'kiskadee, kiskadee, kiskadee ...' – it was the little kiskadee bird, who seemed to be singing to *me*. The whole island had an appearance of being light, cheerful, carefree and warm. I could not believe that I was actually on the fairytale island to which, so often, I had dreamt of running away when I was depressed at school.

For the two weeks that I was in Bermuda I was really happy, a happiness I had not known before. I did things which I had never done before, like going on the back of Kathie's moped, and drinking rum and coke! When I was there Kathie, Peter and Joy treated me as if I did not have anorexia; serving steak and wine, taking me out for meals, to parties and picnics on the warm sand. It was really helpful for people not to be looking at what I was eating all the time and to allow me to be just like them. The foods that I was served would have frightened me back at home, but having them offered in the context of a relaxed atmosphere where I felt special and accepted made me more inclined to eat them. I could let go of my rigid routine and rituals surrounding eating because I was in a completely different environment. The house was full of laughter as Peter played practical jokes and was such a comedian. I saw a side to life I had never really seen: life was fun!

The time went too quickly and a part of me wanted to stay in this world of sun, friendship and laughter. As the holiday progressed I found myself changing so that when I returned I had gained another measure of self-confidence and could laugh again, whereas before it was an effort even to smile.

Another significant change which had taken place in Bermuda was that I had started to menstruate again.

Usually this takes place only when a fair amount of body weight has been maintained for some time. I was about 7 stone 2 pounds and yet my periods had returned. People had been praying for me, particularly that my ability to have children would not be affected. I am sure it was prayer which made the difference, but a part of me was also convinced it was the steak and red wine!

The first thing to confront me on my return was the college examination in which, to my surprise, I did well. In general I began to take more interest in life. I did not feel so divorced from people, began to mix more easily and occasionally socialised in the evenings, which I am sure was in part due to my experiences in Bermuda where, with Peter's witty jokes, I had learned to laugh and talk more easily.

As I became able to mix more easily with the other course members and take more interest in life around me, others seemed to notice that I was there. I felt my personality, which had appeared flat and non-existent, starting to develop. I began to feel that I was a person in my own right. People then started to ask me about my experience with anorexia and I was able to talk about it and face it squarely, which I had not previously been able to do.

Having returned from Bermuda, I realised that the relaxed atmosphere I had been living in had brought changes in my feelings towards food. I no longer suffered from nausea and although I was never very physically hungry I had an appetite for certain types of food. The continuous festivity, going out to meals with food beautifully cooked and presented, and the frequent barbecues with all the fun and effort needed, had made eating more pleasurable. This, I am sure, helped me in the summer term when I went out on work experience with two other girls from my course to a small wine bar in my home town. We got on very well with the owners and people working there. Sometimes we worked during the day and sometimes in the evening, both cooking and serving. It was good experience and great fun.

The main problem with social eating (as well as still eating the inside of bread rolls!) was that I found I was putting on weight much faster than I would have liked. I looked at my new body with disgust. I was 7 stone 7 pounds and felt extremely uncomfortable. Whenever I tried new clothes on they did not fit. The clothes I had were tight and I felt that when I leant over rolls of fat were hanging over the top of my jeans; they clung to my legs which were no longer straight like sticks but bulged out at the top – 'a horrible, horrible sight,' I thought. It did not occur to me to buy larger clothes because I still believed that the clothes were right for me: I was convinced that it was *me* that needed to change, not my clothes! I could not accept my developing body; I could not cope alone. My mind and my body were not compatible.

For the following six weeks I worked as a commis chef at a hotel in Bournemouth. It successfully put me off wanting to go into catering as a career! But it was very good experience and proved beneficial in my second year at college. It was extremely hard work, the hours were long and unsociable and the constant handling of food hard to cope with. Being concerned with food all day and quite often having to face the less pleasant tasks of having to mop up meat juice that had turned sour, with the heat releasing the most appalling odour, nauseated me. The last thing I wanted to do was eat. I think that if it had not been for the support of the people with whom I was staying I could easily have lost weight.

When I finished work at Bournemouth, I went youth hostelling in France with my boyfriend, Andy, with whom I had resumed a good friendship during my first year at college. My eighteenth birthday was coming up, and instead of a party I had chosen to go travelling with Andy. We had a lovely time catching trains, staying in various places right from the north to the south coast. The freedom and independence really helped me.

I returned to college for my final year a far more healthy and confident person. I sensed that people's reactions towards me were completely different from what they had been previously. I was no longer stared at, I was brought into conversations and people asked my opinion about topics rather than ignoring me. I felt more like one of the others. I enjoyed the second year even more than the first year. My main aim was to be conscientious and to use my capabilities to the full. I ensured that I remained near the top of the class in all subjects, to satisfy myself if no one else.

Maintaining a high standard of work was not difficult. The only thing that was a major problem was having to struggle with the psychological aspect of anorexia which had run away with me and was destined to disrupt my life. I lived in hatred of my woman-shaped body, because no one had helped me to accept it.

The last time I had weighed myself I had been 7 stone 7 pounds; I dreaded putting on more weight and feared that I would never be able to stop gaining weight. Consequently I refused to weigh myself; I could not face reality. I still disposed of my sandwiches at college and quite often spent part of the afternoon feeling faint, dizzy or with a bad headache because I had not eaten. When I was alone I had bursts of uncontrollable eating which left me feeling bloated, guilty and shocked at what I had done. I hated myself because I had no self-discipline and no self-respect. I felt stuffed, unclean, dirty and savage.

To relieve me of these feelings and to cleanse my body, in desperation I started taking large doses of laxatives – a miserable, degrading and self-destructive thing to do. It was probably because of the mineral depletion as a result of the laxative abuse that at times I experienced a terrible pain in my bones, especially those in my legs. At night I would lie awake in agony. My weight remained steady but my abnormal attitude towards food and my body haunted me. This adversely affected relationships. I was very sensitive to other people's remarks about my eating habits or weight. I was very touchy, even short-tempered, with my parents, in particular my father to whom I was rather cold and always on the defensive. If I was offered food other than at mealtimes I regarded it as a subtle way of wanting to fatten me up. I was experiencing mental torture – something that I would never wish to go through again.

I kept in touch with one of the nurses who had been working on Adelaide Ward for most of the time that I was in hospital. Everyone around me looked at how much I had changed physically but knew nothing of the agony inside me. I wrote to her in the hope that she would understand what I was going through. She replied:

It is so easy to bluff your way through life kidding everyone that things are fine – unfortunately you can't fool yourself. The main thing to realise is that there is no miracle cure: it can take years for you to recover fully and enjoy food again, so a great deal of perseverance and considerable support will help you. There are so many people who don't understand anorexia, I think it would be helpful if you went to a doctor who is realistic and doesn't fob you off. He will keep you on an even keel, and if you find yourself losing weight you will feel yourself letting him down. Don't feel you are alone, crazy or abnormal; don't expect a miracle; just don't give up.

Her letters often helped me to feel supported, but I knew that I could not do what she was suggesting. How could I go to a doctor? No one I had met *really* understood. I did not want someone merely checking my weight: I wanted someone to help me overcome the self-loathing and to teach me how to eat without losing control. I wanted someone who knew what was going on inside my head and understood the fear and pain. I had become so secretive, not just about food but about so many things. A part of me wanted to talk, but who to and how?

17 | *SOMETIMES I FEEL SO INSECURE*

My eyes sink back
Into deep, dark holes
As a stream of tears
Trickles down my saddened face.

A sharp pain shoots
Through my lifeless body,
Ripping my heart
And piercing my head.

I clench my jaw
To lock the tears
And stare into space,
My eyes a translucent glaze.

My grip gives way
To an outburst of water,
Flooding my childlike body.
Sometimes I feel so insecure.

(Aged 15)

My time as a commis chef in Bournemouth had provided useful experience, not only for my OND course but also of life – some good and some unpleasant. Nearly being raped by the second chef and the heat and hard work in the hotel kitchens in a hot summer contrasted with the very great kindness of the two church families who had me to stay during those weeks. I began to see how life out in the world has its dark and light sides, equally as much as in hospital or school.

It was while I was in Bournemouth that I came across an article about anorexia and an organisation called SARA (the Society for the Advancement of Research into Anorexia), which was helping people with anorexia by raising money for research into the illness. (This charity is no longer in existence.) Apart from a very small article, I had never read anything on anorexia or met anyone else who was suffering. With my maturing attitude to life I was beginning to look outwards and have a greater desire both to do more research into this mystifying condition and to help others. I therefore sent a donation and became a member. The leaflet quoted below spoke clearly to me, although at that time I did not realise what far-reaching effects it would have upon my life.

Anorexia can and does kill. Do you know:

- *Anorexia is a illness of the mind and body. It is an eating disorder often accompanied by profound fear of normal weight. Severe wasting and loss of periods are characteristic.*
- *It is far too common. A specialist has estimated that one in two hundred young women suffers from it. About one in ten anorexics is male. This incidence is comparable with that of diabetes. Older people suffer from it too.*
- *Sufferers can't just 'snap out of it.' An average case can take five years. Many never fully recover.*
- *No one knows how it starts or why a patient recovers. Yet little balanced research is being done.*
- *Successful specialist treatment is seldom available.*
- *SARA hopes to save.*

The Society for the Advancement of Research into Anorexia is a registered charity committed:

- *To promote thorough research into this illness, to discover its causes, to find the best forms of treatment and to establish means of early diagnosis. Thus years of distress can be prevented.*
- *To instigate more and better facilities for specialist treatment, including sustained follow-up care.*
- *To encourage general understanding and awareness of anorexia, so to reduce the extended suffering of patients and their families.*

In February I decided that the one thing I wanted to do was to prevent other people suffering in the way in which I had. Even if I was not completely over anorexia, I could not bear to see other young girls going through the same agony. I wrote to the founder of SARA to find out about setting up a local branch. She agreed to my establishing the first branch and told me what this involved. On 1 May 1982, Berkshire SARA was launched at a buffet supper attended by medics, heads of schools and the general public. Part of the press coverage read:

Now at 18 years old Helena can look at anorexia objectively and say that she is better, if not cured. Now with the pain and anguish of starving to death at least partially behind her, her main aim is to help other sufferers and hopefully prevent more people from falling victim to the illness.

The new branch was launched this month in Reading when Clare Jones, one of the original members of SARA, came to Berkshire to help Helena explain to people the facts about anorexia.

I was pleased that I had done something positive and that

I had something definite to work for – raising funds for research to take place. To me, equally important to raising money, was to enlighten the general public about the complexities of anorexia, or as Nicola Gannon, the newspaper reporter of the above article once said, 'To bring anorexia out of the cupboard and on to the stage.'

More and more I realised how little the general public understood the illness and how little sympathy it gained. Too often it is thought of as self-imposed and concerned only with dieting teenagers who ought to 'snap out of it' and 'pull themselves together', when really it is a callous condition which destroys the sufferer and the morale of the family. Knowing that so many people's view of anorexia was distorted, and seeing the degree of impatience that it elicits, saddened and even angered me. My determination to prove otherwise became so strong that my self-confidence increased and when asked, I was able to talk about anorexia to the public, to the press and on the radio.

It was at that stage that I started to write *Puppet on a String*. During the time I was in hospital I kept an illustrated diary which the nurses and patients loved to read. Several of the nurses said I should have it published. I did not give it a second thought until this time, when I decided that I wanted to write a little more than just my hospital diary, so *Puppet on a String* evolved. I felt compelled to write my experiences and thoughts down on paper to get them off my mind, but to begin with I did not intend it to be published. It was more a way of me working through why I had anorexia. However, as the months went by I knew that what I was writing was to be published so that people could see anorexia from the *inside*.

I also knew that the message I had to get across was one of personal experience, and so a book of this type is not the place in which one can go in depth into the many theories of the causes of anorexia. It seems to me that there is considerable confusion and often difficulty, not only in deciding on the cause and therefore what treatment to administer, but also in diagnosing the illness in its early stages.

I have already expressed a number of my views over the causes, but to summarise the information very briefly, this is what I consider happens. An individual is put under *pressure*. Whether this is from unresolved emotional conflicts, pressure to lose weight, emphasis on success and high standards of achievement, or whether it is sexual pressure leading to an aversion to growing up, this puts the individual under *stress*. Stress in itself can lead to hormonal changes which result in a lack of appetite and weight loss as well as the need to control the appetite, when it is there, in order to feel a sense of power when normally the person feels so powerless. Not until the emotional reasons behind anorexia are sorted will the symptoms of anorexia go. My understanding of anorexia was simple, but I knew that I understood what it *felt* like and that this was important if I were to be used to speak out about the subject.

As well as putting time into SARA I also had to put a lot of energy into college work. Every day the subjects became more intense and my finals crept closer. I did not know what I wanted to do when the course ended. I decided not to worry about what the future held but to concentrate on doing well in my finals. Unlike my school exams, which I could not face and was terrified of taking, I actually quite enjoyed sitting my OND and other college exams.

A week after college ended – I was sad to leave – I started a job at St George's House in Windsor Castle, where my godfather was the warden. I was filling in for one of the cooks for a month. It was a fantastic experience and a good reference to have, but was physically exhausting and did not help my fight against anorexia.

I shared a flat with the other cook, in the castle grounds.

We started work at 7.20 am, making bread, then sat down for something to eat before preparing breakfast and lunch for the thirty-odd conference guests. This usually took us to about 1.00 pm, when there was a mad rush to have all the food dished up and in the hotplate or oven, and to clear away and wash the equipment. If I had wanted to I could have sat down to a meal at lunchtime, but after dealing with food all morning I could not face eating it so I very rarely ate lunch. Between 2.00 pm and 4.00 pm we were off duty. More often than not I sat outside in the sun to take the weight off my feet. The afternoons and evenings were always hectic, running around getting everything ready in time for dinner and doing as much preparation for the next day as possible. By the time work ended about 8.00 pm I was too tired to want to eat; I was not hungry, but sometimes made myself have a meal because I knew what would happen if I did not.

In the evenings I used to read, write or listen to music, or go out to the pub or fair with some of the domestic assistants and nannies from Windsor Castle. We had great fun. I felt even more exhilarated when coming back to the castle in the early hours of the morning, approaching the huge overpowering doors and showing identification to the policeman. We would hear the clunk of the bolt and then walk in. The huge stone walls on either side were lit up by lamps and shone a mysterious gold, warm and welcoming but at the same time uncanny. As we walked, one of the guards marched up and down, obviously keeping a watchful eye on us. We passed under an archway which led into the Horseshoe Cloisters, past the entrance to St George's Chapel, with the grand steps gracefully leading up to the ornate door on to which a golden light was thrown, and through another archway which led to St George's House. It sounds all so exciting, but we often paid a price for our fun – only four hours sleep before a heavy day's work.

After about two weeks I found myself attacked by the

same feelings of despair and depression with which I had so often struggled at school, feelings which I had not experienced since I came out of hospital. I had been unhappy at times, but not come up against this deep sense of loneliness and desperation. As I had done before, I began questioning every aspect of life. When I was alone I cried quietly; once more I stared into the mirror and saw a miserable face, dejected and full of pain. I could not understand why there was such agony behind those tear-stricken eyes – my eyes. It was not so much unhappiness that I felt, but intense emotional anguish; inconsolable grief.

At the time, it made no sense to me. I thought people only hurt if something happened to them, but looking back I can see that perhaps it was tied in with years of suppressed pain, my inability to communicate and relate, self-consciousness, lack of assertiveness and simply not knowing how to handle life, people or myself. My pain was to do with not knowing how to cope in life and with unhealed hurts, but because I thought that nothing had happened to cause my pain I decided I could not tell anyone about it, in fear that they thought I was making it up or was 'mad'.

On the occasions that my mother came over to see me at Windsor Castle, she was convinced that I was losing weight and looking unwell and for this reason visited me far more than she would otherwise have done. The last three days brought the end-of-season cleaning up. We worked through the whole day for several days in succession, and by the end I was worn out.

18 | CHANGED

My life has changed
Into something new,
My thoughts rearranged
Since I knew you.

Good has grown from bad
And beauty is all I see,
Even when I am sad
Or pain takes hold of me.

(Aged 19)

The end of the summer brought with it an intense emotional experience, with love and pain intertwined, which had a dramatic effect on me and changed my whole perception of life.

After finishing work at Windsor Castle, as a last minute decision I had agreed to join one of my ex-school friends, Mary, to do a week's voluntary work as a cook at the CYFA (Christian Youth Fellowship Association) camp in Limpsfield, Surrey.

Mary was one of the few people from school that I had remained in contact with. She was one of the two girls who arrived a term late in my first year at boarding school and she too was bullied. She had been born with dislocated hips and walked with a limp, which the other girls laughed at. The girls used to make her crawl on her hands and knees to go to the loo in the night and would kick her in the bladder as she went. To this day she still has bladder problems as a result.

We arrived at the large old building situated in an expanse of land. As we walked across the driveway towards the front door the sky hung dark over our heads; there was a bite to the air and it was raining. As we entered the building and went up the stairs to our dormitory my mind was filled with too many less favourable memories of school for comfort. Despite the excitement of the work and meetings which lay ahead, I could already feel the sword of pain cutting its way through my body, but I covered up my feelings, which I felt were inane.

The following day was a bustle of activity as the house-party arrived, comprised of around a hundred teenagers.

I soon became familiar with the surroundings and accustomed to the routine, which put me more at ease. There were about eight cooks and several pantry staff, all carefully arranged so that no one missed either the morning or evening meetings. The meetings were a real inspiration to me and their message became more wonderful each time. We usually started off by singing several choruses from *Youth Praise* or a similar song book which was quite often followed by a sketch acted by a few senior members, illustrating an important point or passage in the Bible. Then there was always a talk given by one of the leaders, with prayers and songs bringing the meeting to a close.

Over the previous two years I had become distant from God and even my attending church held no special meaning. I had not even taken a Bible to the camp with me, yet each time I walked into the meeting room I felt a yearning in myself for something just out of my reach. I was deeply moved by the songs we sang, and also by the talks and the amazing love – God's love – which radiated from so many people there. I cried tears from my heart to feel the presence of such a wonderful love. An agony flowed through my body as I longed to know this love and for it to fill my heart. Yet I was filled with fear; there was no room for love.

Working in the kitchen during much of the day did not detract from the special moments encountered during the meetings. While preparing the food there was much fellowship; we shared among ourselves our reason for belief in God, what He had done in our lives, what the meeting had meant to us that morning, our problems and difficulties, and far more. During the middle of the morning the pantry staff made coffee and joined the rest of us in the kitchen for a time of prayer and the sharing of a passage from the Bible. If we happened to be extremely busy at that moment then we would make up for the prayer time later, or give our profound apologies to God!

One of the nicest things about working in the kitchen at Limpsfield was the incredible atmosphere. It was free of the pressures I had experienced elsewhere, and the people cared about each other. There was trust, joy and excitement, rather than constant anxiety. It was nothing unusual to be cooking and singing a chorus at the same time. I remember on one occasion making fruit salad and joining in with a chorus, and each time I went to collect more fruit from the room next door, where the boys were peeling potatoes, I came back singing the song they were singing!

However, I was still finding eating extremely difficult and being at Limpsfield was no exception. As soon as it was time to eat, an intense fear would flood through my body, my stomach would be tied up in knots, I would literally be shaking and could not bring myself to enter the dining room. The noise of a hundred people munching food, the thought of eating three meals a day and having to face food when I had no appetite, was too much. I think I was at the stage where, given the circumstances, I could have gone right back to square one in anorexia. I had not experienced such a profound fear over eating for a long time and my revulsion towards food, my lack of appetite and hunger and the way in which my stomach tensed up at the thought of eating were exactly the same feelings as those experienced just before I went into hospital. Thankfully I was at the right place to halt me in my tracks and I believe there was a definite purpose behind my going through these feelings again, one which God could use for good.

In a moment of desperation I explained my eating difficulties to someone else working in the kitchen. Although she did not understand anorexia, Sue was a great help and very nobly spent several mealtimes in the kitchen with me so that I could eat as much or as little as I liked. We often spent the time talking about God, Jesus and the Bible as I tried to grasp the real meaning of faith and its importance.

Another person who helped me a great deal was Paula. She was a really caring person who had had her fair share of depression and anxiety. Through having suffered in this way, she understood the mental anguish I was experiencing and we often went on long walks through the woods discussing the problem. Wandering among the tall, graceful trees and tangled undergrowth, the sun setting in the distance, casting its golden light upon the path, something Paula had emphasised came back to me again and again:

God wants to set you free, because He loves you as an individual.

The freedom which she spoke of was not just freedom from anorexia but complete freedom to be oneself; not to have that feeling of being tied down and trapped. I could not fully comprehend such freedom, but I longed for it. Yet I did not feel that I personally could experience such a thing. My confusion began to override my aspirations.

Once more people surged into the dining room for supper. Suddenly, I became panic-stricken and at the same time nauseated by the smell of the food. In terror, I ran upstairs. Safe from food I had time to calm down and gather my thoughts a little. I stood staring out of the window, supporting my weight on its ledge. The sky was grey and oppressive, the landscape drab. A sheet of mist hung in front of the woods and hills, tree-tops faded into the skyline from which a drizzling rain fell. I had my note-book at hand and was recalling one of the talks given a few days previously. One aspect in particular stuck in my mind, 'The closer you get to Jesus, the closer you get to other people.' I tried to illustrate the idea in sketch form; I paused for a moment. The door opened and Paula walked in.

'I thought you'd be here,' she said. I carried on writing and sketching my thoughts. She looked over my shoulder at what I had done.

'What you have written is very true,' she said warmly. 'You do get closer to other people. But we have to learn to love ourselves first, because we are told in the Commandments to love God with all our heart. If our hearts are filled with hatred of ourselves, we can't love God fully. Then we are told to love our neighbour as ourselves. If we hate ourselves, we hate our neighbour. So before anything else we have to learn to accept ourselves.'

'How can I love myself to the degree you're talking about whilst I still have anorexia?' I asked. 'It's a deceitful, secretive illness. I can only feel guilty and hate myself for the things I do. But at the same time I can't control it. It's something you can't just snap out of – it's an illness.'

'I know, but God can help you. Remember in Philippians 4:6 it says, "Don't worry about anything, but in all your prayers ask God for what you need."'

I looked down at the piece of paper on which I had been doodling. 'You probably won't understand this, Paula, but I'm scared of getting better.'

'I do understand,' she replied gently. 'You have a lot to be scared of. It can't be an easy problem to overcome, but offer it to God and you will no longer be frightened. He loves you. "There is no fear in love; perfect love drives out all fear" (1 John 4:18). Shall we go somewhere quiet and pray?'

'Yes,' I replied.

'God loves you Helena,' Paula had said. The more I thought about those few words, the more wonderful they seemed to be. Realising that, "We love because God first loved us" (1 John 4:19) made things even clearer. Because God loves us, we are able to love ourselves.

Everything appeared to be linking up now. The missing piece to the puzzle had been found and I was now able to see the connection.

> GOD loves YOU
> which enables
> YOU to love YOURSELF
> you can then love
> OTHERS as YOURSELF
> and therefore love
> GOD
> with all your heart

Later I was reading the Bible and discovered a passage which summed up everything I was learning about God and love. Love comes from God. "Dear friends, let us love one another, because love comes from God. Whoever loves is a child of God and knows God" (1 John 4:7).

The passage continues: "If this is how God loved us, then we should love one another. No one has ever seen God, but if we love one another, God lives in union with us, and his love is made perfect in us" (1 John 4:11-12).

One evening, while the house party was gathered in the old wood-panelled dining room having supper, I stood talking to Sue. She was trying to explain how great God's love is for us and how He longs for us fully to accept Him into our lives.

'Just remember that God is standing there knocking on your door; you've only got to invite Him in,' she told me.

From other talks during the week I had also learned that there was a big gap between God and people, and that the only way the gap could be filled was through Jesus standing in between, because Jesus came and died for us. The only way we have a restored relationship with God is through Jesus. Jesus stands between us and God, and when God looks at us He sees us like Jesus.

I spent virtually the whole of that night and the following day thinking about what Sue had said. I realised that my life was like a house and that God was standing and knocking on the door, but that throughout my life I had been conversing with God through the letterbox. Not once, when I knew very well that He was out there, or even when He knocked, had I opened the door and invited Him in. There was a hidden reason as to why I always kept the door closed between us: inside, my house was in a terrible mess; it needed a thorough clean before I could possibly let Him in. By the time evening came I had actually grasped the fact that God does not mind how bad the mess inside our house is. It is His work and pleasure to help us clear it up, and through allowing Him to do so we are changed into better people.

Suddenly my heart overflowed with a never-ending warmth. I knew, at that moment, that Jesus was knocking at my door, but this time I really wanted to open it wide and let Him inside, and so I did; I asked Jesus to be Lord of my life. I wanted to tell God that I believed in Him, and I believed that He sent His Son Jesus to earth and that Jesus died so that I could have eternal life. But not only did I believe it – now it made sense! I leapt with joy, and bubbling over with excitement I rushed to Sue's room to tell her the news.

'That's wonderful, Helena,' she said, her eyes shining with delight. I was so happy I could not stop smiling; nor could Sue.

'Shall we pray together?' I said.

'Yes,' she replied, grasping my hand.

The faith in the few words that she spoke was tremendous, 'Oh Father! Thank You that Helena wants to let You into her heart.' I felt a vibration pass through her hands into mine. I wanted God's love to grow and grow in my heart.

'Have you got a Bible?' she asked.

'Not a modern one,' I said.

'Right, let's go and get one then! The cooks are allowed a free book; let's go and fetch yours now.'

We ran down the stairs, along the corridor and into the library where I picked my very own Bible.

Just before I went to sleep that night, I opened my Bible at random. The picture which lay in front of me was the feeding of the five thousand, a parable I knew well, but this time I understood something personal that I am sure God was telling me. Here were five thousand people who had nothing to eat and through a miracle of Jesus all were fed and their hearts were filled with gratitude. I had food enough to satisfy my hunger, far more than they, but I rejected it; there was no gratitude in my heart. I was too concerned with myself.

I glanced at the passage below the picture.

If anyone wants to come with me, he must forget self, take up his cross every day, and follow me. For whoever wants to save his own life will lose it, but whoever loses his life for my sake will save it. Will a person gain anything if he wins the whole world but is himself lost or defeated? Of course not! (Luke 9:23-25).

I think God was teaching me through that passage the importance of humility, and also that His path is the hardest to follow but the only one with treasure worth having at the end. He was also showing me that through anorexia I had been concerned only with myself and that my anorexia had robbed me because it had become my whole life.

In the morning I felt excited and overjoyed at my new

discoveries about God and changed feelings towards life.

During each of the remaining days Sue and I spent half an hour reading a passage from the Bible, finding out its meaning and relevance to our lives. I was hungry for God's Word and gained a great deal from these studies. As I was getting to know God better and asking Him to help me more, I could sense Him working deeply in my life. I was not only hungry for the Word of God, but also for food! Very gradually my appetite was returning, fear was losing its grip and tension was calming down. I was able to enter the dining room to eat a full meal and my stomach even started to have hunger pangs again. As well as being a miracle it was a wonderful feeling!

One evening I was talking to Nicky, a friend I had made a few days previously at Limpsfield. She had a gentle and caring attitude and her eyes shone brilliantly whenever she spoke of God. She had been asking me about anorexia and explaining what happiness I could find in life if only I could get over the illness.

'One thing I pray for you, Helena, is that you find a really good friend when you get back home.'

She had her guitar with her and was quietly strumming a few chords. She suggested that we went somewhere quiet and sang some songs. A group of us, including Paula and my school friend Mary, sat on the step to the chapel, and the others on the floor in front. The chapel was dimly lit with a golden light which was warm and welcoming. I felt so content in the beautifully peaceful atmosphere. As we sang quietly to the music of the guitar the room was filled with love. Everyone sang with such meaning and the words of the songs moved me deeply. Suddenly I felt a pain shoot through my body: it was as though I were being torn to shreds. I stared straight ahead, and tears rolled down my cheeks. I could see Jesus suffering on the cross; what agony he experienced.

Nicky put her arm round me. 'Is there anything you want to sing, Helena?' she whispered.

'"Jesus take me as I am; I can come no other way",' I replied.

It was a chorus I had just learnt and the words moved me deeply. I really wanted Jesus to take me. He died to save me.

When we had finished singing everyone left the chapel except for Nicky, Paula, Carrie and me.

'Do you really want to know Jesus?' Nicky asked me.

'Yes,' I replied. 'I love Him.' My voice was full of pain.

'Pray then, Helena,' Nicky gently urged.

'I can't.'

Paula took hold of my hand. 'Do you want us to pray for you, Helena?'

'Yes please.'

They all laid hands on me and prayed.

Two days later the camp drew to a close. My time there had been one of intense pain intertwined with awe and wonder; a time for searching for new realisations. Above all else, I had discovered the meaning to life. I said goodbye to Limpsfield with the knowledge that there would always be Someone with me through both the rough and the smooth. Just as I was leaving, Paula gave me a book called *Love Yourself*, about self-acceptance and depression. Sue gave me a passage to look up in the Bible: "So I am sure that God, who began this good work in you, will carry it on until it is finished" (Philippians 1:6).

I had so much to say thank you for – even more so when my mother came to pick me up. As we set off home I opened my post, which she had brought with her. The first letter I opened was my Diploma result – it was a pass. I was pleased that I had attained a diploma, but very disappointed that it was not a distinction. I had apparently only been short of a few marks in just one subject, otherwise I would have obtained a distinction. I went on ripping open the envelopes and half-heartedly reading the contents. I had a shock when I read one of the letters.

'Hey Mum! Listen to this,' I said in a tone of amazement. '"Dear Ms Wilkinson, you have been judged by a distinguished panel of seven experts to be the winner in the student category of the Leverclean Award 1982 – congratulations. The presentation of your £500 prize will…"'

'Hang on a second, let me stop the car and have a look at this,' my mother interrupted.

I showed her the letter and she went on to read about the presentation dinner in London.

It was a national competition that had been open to catering students and professional caterers. A few weeks before we were due to take our finals at college, one of the tutors had asked us to enter the competition. Rather reluctantly we did. A fortnight later we all received a pen through the post with compliments of Lever Industrial. 'A subtle way of saying that you haven't come anywhere,' I thought. Two months later I realised my thoughts were wrong! I was overwhelmed and so was my tutor!

It was a marvellous end to the very special time I had spent in Limpsfield. I was filled with happiness; life was so exciting, there was such a lot to learn and so much to explore.

19 | *IN CAPTIVITY*

She cannot escape
From bars in the cage,
Shut in for hours
Her mind in a rage.

Her heart is cold
And emotions none,
She tries to be bold
But life's no fun.

She dreams each day
Of hills and mountains,
How she'd fly away
Towards crystal fountains.

The world outside
Is bright and gay,
Like a leaping tide
Is how she should stay.

Not in a dark drab room
Cold and bare,
Full of gloom
But open in the air.

Fly to the place
I've loved so long,
Soar up with grace
And sing my song.

Let me live and love
And be free to do,
Like any other dove
What she wishes to.

(Aged 17)

The first Sunday back at home I had arranged to meet Sue's sister, Helen, who lived quite near me. She was going to introduce me to Greyfriars church, which she attended. We went along to both the morning and evening services and she then introduced me to Crossroads, the young people's group which met to sing, pray, study the Bible and talk about relevant issues concerning young people. There was a lovely atmosphere and I knew that I had found something very special. Afterwards I was offered a lift home since the church was not in my home town and public transport was somewhat unsafe at that time of night. I found myself squashed up in the back of a mini with another girl, and a guitar across our laps pinning us firmly to the seat. Tania introduced herself and we started chatting. She was an easy-going kind of person and so conversation flowed. We then drove past the sign to the Royal Berkshire Hospital and by our reactions we discovered that we had both been in there! She went on to explain that she had had to have an operation on her arm after a cycling accident.

'What were you in the Royal Berks for?' she asked.

'Anorexia,' I replied.

She put her hand out to mine and shook it. 'Snap!'

God certainly moves in a mysterious way. The friend Nicky had prayed that I would find was pinned to the back seat of a mini with me. I could not have found a more ideal friend if I had tried; a Christian who had beaten anorexia! Even more amazing was that not only had she been anorexic and was going to the same church as me, but our parents lived in the same town! What more could I have wanted? We exchanged addresses and arranged to meet the next day.

The following day we sat talking over a cup of coffee. First, we enlightened each other on what we were doing: she was taking A levels at school and wanted to go on to read medicine at university. Then our conversation turned to the inevitable – anorexia. She asked me about my experiences and how I felt now. It was so encouraging to talk to someone who had come through the illness. My anguish was once hers and she knew only too well what I was talking about. She went on to ask me how important a part my faith played in my recovery and posed a question which made me think very deeply about the situation.

'Do you want Jesus as your hero?'

'Yes I do,' I replied.

'What you do to your body you are doing to Jesus.' If you love Him and really want Him, then He will live in you and be a part of you, but by not eating the right things you hurt Him as much as you damage yourself'.

What she said was very true. I realised what she was getting at: if I loved Jesus with all my heart, how could I hurt Him by damaging myself? To a degree I understood how to overcome the psychological side of anorexia, but what about the physical side? How does one overcome not being hungry, revulsion at the sight of food, and nausea?

'Jesus died to save us suffering,' Tania explained. 'Our agony is His; He bears our burdens. In other words He can take from us our fears and illnesses if only we are prepared to let Him help us. We should be living our lives in glory for God. We can't do that if we are heavily laden with fear.'

I realised that there are three dimensions to overcoming anorexia: physical, psychological and spiritual. The one dimension that I had neglected was the spiritual – the most important aspect of all. As Tania said, 'Jesus can take from us our fears and illnesses.'

A few days later Tania came round to my house after school. We had hardly known each other, yet we had so much to say and so much to share. She asked if she could read some of my poetry. I handed her a selection. There was silence. She looked up at me from where she was sitting cross-legged on the floor.

'I've never been moved to tears by poetry before.'

She picked up one of my latest poems *In Captivity*. 'You really are in captivity, aren't you?'

I had not realised that the poem reflected my feelings so much. My agony of feeling trapped in anorexia was portrayed through the agony of a captive dove. I knew that I was almost over the anorexia, but there was still something holding me in the anorexic way of thinking and I wanted to be totally free.

Tania mentioned that she had been very much helped by a doctor in Oxford and that I ought to make an appointment to see him.

'It may seem a long way to go, but I'm sure you'd travel to Timbuktu to get better. When I had it, I certainly did,' she said.

I told her I did not consider myself sufficiently ill to see a doctor.

'You might think that you're better physically, but I can tell that psychologically you're nowhere near cured. Please get in touch with Doctor P.J.'

She later sent me two passages from the Bible to look up, to keep my focus God:

He helps us in all our troubles, so that we are able to help others who have all kinds of troubles, using the same help that we ourselves have received from God.

(2 Corinthians 1:4)

'Keep up the good work!' she said.

> Happy is the person who remains faithful under trials, because when he succeeds in passing such a test, he will receive as his reward the life which God has promised to those who love him (James 1:12).

She finished, 'Well! I've been through it; I pray I can help you, Helena.'

At first, I couldn't find the motivation and courage to contact the doctor. Yet deep down I knew anorexia still had a hold on my life.

I was struggling with a psychological battle. I was on the defensive with people, and felt as though the world hated me. This feeling of being hated did not turn into rejection, but a need to search to understand the meaning of life. In my need I turned to the Bible for reassurance.

> If the world hates you, just remember that it has hated me first. If you belonged to the world, then the world would love you as its own. But I chose you from this world, and you do not belong to it; that is why the world hates you (John 15:18-19).

One night I felt so dispirited that I decided to ring Tania and ask if I could go over and talk to her. We chatted for a couple of hours drinking endless cups of tea. We talked about both serious and crazy things; we laughed and almost cried. Throughout the evening the pain in the bones of my legs increased, becoming agonising. 'If only the whole illness could be behind me,' I thought. I looked at Tania, full of life, full of praise for how wonderful life is.

'When I had anorexia,' she said 'life was terrible and I was so boring! Look at me now – well, maybe don't! I can really enjoy life, it's such fun.'

I glanced at her enviously as I noticed the difference between us.

'Don't you want to enjoy life again, Helena?'

I sighed heavily. 'Yes! I do.'

'Let's go and phone Doctor P.J. now,' she said.

I sat and waited whilst Tania spoke to him. Everything was arranged: all I had to do was to ring up the following day to make an appointment with him.

Then the moment of truth came, the initial consultation with Dr P.J. He saw my parents and me together first to establish the background of my illness and their reactions to it. Then he spent quite a long time discussing the problem with me alone. He asked how I felt now, about my eating patterns and my attitude towards my body and weight.

Then he suggested that I was weighed. I dreaded the thought; I had avoided weighing myself for over a year. He asked how much I thought I weighed. I said about 7 stone 7 pounds; it was a wild guess and wishful thinking. I could not accept that I would be over 8 stone; 7 stone 7 pounds sounded an OK weight to me, and I thought, 'Please, please, let it be 7 stone 7 pounds.' I stood on the scales. My weight was over 8 stone, something I had lived in fear of for the past five years. The thought repelled me. Even if I were a little under the average weight for my age and height, it was only a matter of pounds and I felt terrible.

The main thing that Dr P.J. was concerned about was that I had at last faced reality. Nevertheless, I left the consultation feeling very disheartened.

I arranged to see him once a month for an hour, when we would work through the problem together. In the short time I had spoken to him I knew that I had come to the right person. He was realistic and concerned with treating not only the illness but the person as a whole, which I knew was essential.

A couple of weeks later I was asked if I could return to St George's House in Windsor Castle for about a month, as one of the cooks was ill. This time I stayed with my godparents as opposed to sharing the flat with the other cook. However, for the first two nights I slept in one of the guest rooms in St George's House. After I had finished work on the second day I had a sudden severe attack of depression. In my desperation I fled home. My father had quite a shock when, driving back from work, he saw me wandering along in the dark from the bus stop. He stopped the car and I climbed in. He said that my cousin Kathie had phoned from Bermuda the previous night to remind us of her brother's television programme. I was feeling so low that I decided to phone her back. She suggested I arrange to go over there again. I planned to go out just after Christmas, and I decided I would spend the money I had won in the Leverclean Award on an extended holiday, finishing *Puppet on a String* out there. I stayed at home that night and got up early in the morning to go back to Windsor.

I enjoyed the remaining weeks at St George's House. It was less exhausting than the previous time and we had some interesting people to cook for.

Part way through the month I had my second appointment with Dr P.J. The two aspects which seemed to come out most strongly were self-consciousness and self-acceptance. The conversation began with looking at anxiety and how it affected my eating patterns. On the whole, when I was anxious or worried I lost my appetite and stopped eating. I then told him that I had days when I binged. He asked what I meant by this, and I explained how I started eating one thing and then moved on to another and another. This led on to assessing the kind of mood I was in when I binged, why it happened and how I felt afterwards. I explained my feelings of guilt and revulsion. I confessed that to cope with these feelings I took handfuls of laxatives. He explained that taking laxatives would barely alter my weight, because the food had already been absorbed. It had a mainly psychological effect of relieving my guilt, and in fact could have drastic effects on my body and disrupt the use of my colon and rectum. I was aware of the effects that it was having on my body, because of the pain and discomfort I experienced at times, but until I could establish sensible eating patterns I could not see a way out.

From eating we went on to talk about weight, size, shape and general appearance, discussing the parts of me about which I was self-conscious – my hips and thighs. Dr P.J. said that he could tell that it was that area of my body I was concerned about because of the way in which I hid it underneath big jumpers. I then had to explain my feelings and reactions if I was forced to wear very light clothes. I did this with tremendous difficulty. It was not easy to make such an attempt because it meant facing reality. Whatever I said it always seemed to indicate my inability to accept myself or face reality. My weight had not changed from the previous month.

The time passed so quickly that before I realised it I had finished working at Windsor. I returned home to complete a few Christmas cakes which I had on order and to do some assignments for a correspondence course which I was taking with The Writing School. After a few days at home I felt extremely tired and had sharp pains in my head. In the middle of the night I woke up with a fever and an excruciating pain across my stomach. My parents called the doctor who said it was a gastro-intestinal virus and gave me some painkillers, but I could not stop being sick, so he came back and gave me something else to ease it. Not surprisingly I lost a little weight. However, the fact that I did not continue to lose weight after the virus had gone showed that I was definitely on the road to recovery from anorexia, and had lost the need inside to gain control and power through weight loss.

We had a lovely family Christmas and three days afterwards I flew out to Bermuda for five weeks. Peter, Joy and Kathie were at the airport to meet me. As we drove from St Davids, the island on which the airport is situated, across the causeway and on towards Hamilton, I was filled with exhilaration. I knew that there was a reason for my coming back to this tiny island in the middle of the Atlantic, and it was far more significant than having a holiday and capturing sub-tropical beauties.

The island was more breathtakingly beautiful than I remembered, with its attractively designed houses in a range of pastel colours all capped with their white lime-stone roofs, and gardens a mass of luscious citrus trees and banana plants heavily laden with fruit – a riot of colour. Palm trees gracefully reached towards the skyline; hedgerows overflowed with rich pink hibiscus flowers; the island abounded in deep red poinsettias, contrasting with the spiky green leaves of the Spanish bayonets. The collection of pink sandy beaches; healthy vegetation extending to the beaches' edge and the turquoise blue sea lapping on to its shore is a sight not to be missed. The volcanic rock which juts out of the water in irregular shapes, with fascinating sea-creatures clinging to its sides; the clear blue ocean, which is purple over the coral reefs, filled with a vast selection of fish, including barracuda, yellowtail snappers, wahoo, Bermuda chub, rainbow runners and parrot fish, along with some wonderful underwater creations – these are a world of their own.

The atmosphere was very much one of festivity, with Gombey dancers in their multi-coloured costumes performing in the streets to see in the New Year, and we received numerous invitations to attend 'open house' parties. However enjoyable such times were, I benefited most through simply talking to Kathie. Discussing past situations and consequent pain gave me the opportunity to look at the past objectively and give thought to rela-tionships, in particular those in my immediate family. It enabled me to put the pieces of the puzzle together, to comprehend some of the difficulties, past and present, and where possible to amend the situations.

With my new awareness of relationships and past events, I spent the last few days in Bermuda soaking up the sun in picturesque surroundings, thinking about the question Tania had asked me, 'Do you want to enjoy life again, Helena?' For the first time I *really* wanted to take hold of that 'good life' she spoke of.

20 | *INVISIBLE STRENGTH*

That deep piercing pain
Which burrows into my heart
And dwells in all my body,
Suddenly begins to part.

The intensity is fading
And beauty is intertwined;
An ever-growing love
Calms my restless mind.

How can I explain
This incredible feeling,
When an invisible strength
Gives peace to my whole being.

I need not explain why,
Just let the peace flow through;
Know that God is here
And thank Him in all I do.

(Aged 19)

Helped by the Bermuda sunshine, winter passed quickly back in England and the first sign of spring brought with it new life. Quite by chance I decided to go to the Women's World Day of Prayer. I know I was led there, if only to hear what Joyce, the speaker, had to say.

She began by describing how we might let God into one

room only of our lives. 'After release in the spirit,' she went on, 'it's as if Our Lord says, "I know I am welcome here in this room, but I desire to be Lord of all your house." Panic usually seizes one! One thinks of the rest of the house and the disorder and dismay in the different rooms. However, Jesus says, "Don't be afraid, take my hand and we shall go through your house together." He then says, "We shall start with the attic." This is usually a most disconcerting suggestion and maybe we remonstrate with Jesus, and say – politely, of course – "But Lord, there's so much rubbish and junk up there." "Yes I know," says Jesus, "but take my hand and we'll go together. I quite agree there is junk and we will discard this together, but also there are precious things up there that you don't know about, which I desire for you to use for Me in My Kingdom."

'Jesus continues, "After the attic, may I go into your bedroom? This is the room where images are set in place, where masks are carefully put on. Maybe relationships aren't in My order in this room – do not fear, I am the answer to all problems." He says, "I will teach you to remove your mask and show you that I love and accept you unconditionally, just as you are, and also teach you to love and accept yourself unconditionally, because I do." He asks, "May we go into your kitchen, and may I sit in the corner and listen to all your conversations? May I hear the loving things you say about your family, to your family, and about your neighbours and friends? May I listen to you as you upbuild My body?"

'He then asks, "Do you have a basement?" We truly shudder. "Don't be afraid of the basement in your life – your hidden past, maybe guilt, resentment, fear, anxiety…even dark corners that have no name – don't be afraid. I am the Light of the World and I've taken you out of the darkness. Come, let Me heal all the wounds of your past, as I've promised to bind up all wounds. Will you invite Me to be Lord of every room in your life?"'

On my way home and during the rest of the week, I went over and over Joyce's talk. I thought back to my time at Limpsfield when I opened my 'door' and welcomed God in; how wonderfully happy I felt then, and how glad I was that I had really accepted Him. It seemed amazing that Jesus had taken my hand and was gently leading me through the different rooms. He had already started work on my attic, discarding the rubbish and bringing out the precious things which He desires I use for Him. He had shown me that relationships were not in His order. Above all, He had given me the most fantastic reassurance, that He loved and accepted me unconditionally, and He was also teaching me to love and accept myself – something I had never been able to do in the past. Jesus had moved through so many rooms, tidying, cleaning and polishing them. He had brought healing to so many areas of my life and was so clearly changing me. It was marvellous, the work He was doing, and I really wanted Him to be Lord of my life.

I recalled the question at the end of the talk, 'Will you invite Me to be Lord of *every* room in your life?'

'No! Not my basement,' I thought. 'I've hidden the key. No one enters my basement; it's filled with dark corners and buried pain.' My basement contained some of the deeper scars from childhood and the anger I felt at being partially sighted. It hurt too much to let anyone near these things.

At the end of the week Tania rang me up to see if I would like to go to the service at Greyfriars church on Sunday and then on to Crossroads. It had been over three months since I had gone, and although I liked the church and had received a very warm welcome, I had often felt on the outside and awkward. Nevertheless, I decided it would be nice to go along, especially if we could go together – she seemed to have the ability to mix and relate in a way that I did not, and so being with her rather than on my own made things easier.

I was overwhelmed when I heard Ian's talk at Crossroads; it followed exactly what Joyce had said at the Women's World Day of Prayer service. He spoke about the importance of giving God the key to every room in our house, and my mind was immediately transported to the hidden key of my basement. Ian went on to stress that if we really love God, we must not only give all our keys but give up our old lives and start anew. This can be fulfilled by letting God's Holy Spirit come into us. 'Could God be trying to tell me something?' I thought. It was certainly more than chance that I had attended both meetings. Perhaps God was trying to say that not until I revealed my basement could I be completely cured of anorexia, and that through revealing it my faith would grow. In many ways I wanted to speak to Ian about not being able to hand over my basement to God, but I did not have the courage.

At that moment, Joan, the vicar's wife and a Crossroads leader, came over and said how nice it was to see me again. I appreciated her warm welcome and felt encouraged.

That night I spent several hours considering what to do about my hidden memories and pain. I very much needed to bring them out into the open, I knew that until I had done this I could not be fully cured of anorexia, but the thought of facing those dark corners alone was more than I could bear.

The following afternoon I plucked up courage and decided to go and see Joan. I explained my difficulties and was soon convinced that I had done the right thing in coming. I began to realise that I would not be facing the dark corners alone – Jesus would be beside me in every move I made. I longed for Him to come and walk with me, but I was scared that in handing over my anorexia I would lose self-control, having no control over my body and myself.

Joan explained that God does not take our self-control

from us. We still have control over what we do; God merely offers us an alternative and is there to guide us.

When I arrived home I decided to look up the passage in the Bible which Ian had mentioned at the end of his talk: 'But the Spirit produces love, joy, peace, patience, kindness, goodness, faithfulness, humility and self-control' (Galatians 5:22-23). I leapt with joy when I read the last two words: No, God doesn't take self-control from us; He gives it to us!

The next Sunday at church we sang one of my favourite hymns, 'My song is love unknown.' The words touched me deeply and I felt particularly close to God, yet for some reason I left the church feeling empty and down. I knew that I had to talk and pray with Ian, as Joan had previously suggested. When I arrived the sky was dark and oppressive, and as we discussed the problem the rain fell in heavy sheets. Ian said that he felt my past feelings of rejection, depressions and anorexia were closely linked and asked if I would like him and his wife to pray with me to be released from these things and filled with God's Spirit. I felt happy about their praying for me and afterwards felt warm and tranquil. Up until then I had not understood the Holy Spirit, but began to see how when Jesus died He left us with the Holy Spirit to be at work in the life of those who believe and trust in Him.

I was still having regular consultations with Dr P.J. in Oxford, and each time I saw him after returning from Bermuda he noticed a change for the better in me. When I visited him in March, after talking with Ian, he suggested there should be a longer gap between this and my next consultation, which in fact proved to be my last. The one thing which seemed to come across most strongly to him was the fact that I was now beginning to face reality. The prayer I had received had brought tremendous release and healing, and the weeks in Bermuda and my friendship with Tania had given me the opportunity to be myself; something I began to see was vital. Two people confirmed the importance of this matter. My friend Doris wrote:

> I think you have a most interesting life ahead of you, giving so much of which you have an abundance – sensitivity, experience and artistic talent. I am quite serious about this: just go on being yourself, and having the courage to be yourself. So many people feel that they have to project the image that has been cast for them by family and tradition. I'm not decrying the latter for they have helped to create the person, but to try to express oneself within these confines can be frustrating.

Kathie also told me:

> *Nobody* can destroy *you*: you are who you are, and whatever you do or touch, your stamp is on that. What media you choose to express yourself in is *not* important; what is important is that you are true to yourself in that form of expression.

The fear of letting anorexia go had disappeared and I began to realise that my complete recovery and freedom would be as a result of a process, a journey.

Love was the first thing I had to comprehend. I had spent my time searching for love and security in the things I did, and especially in the people I met. My endless searching was to no avail. Then, one day, I was thumbing through my Bible haphazardly and three words leapt out at me: 'God is love' (1 John 4:8). 'God is love,' I repeated to myself, 'Wow! I've discovered love.'

I went on to read:

> Whoever loves is a child of God and knows God. Whoever does not love does not know God, for God is love. And God showed his love for us by sending his only Son into the world, so that we might have life

through him. This is what love is: it is not that we have loved God, but that he loved us and sent his Son to be the means by which our sins are forgiven.

(1 John 4:7-10)

I knew that I had found something extremely precious; not only the meaning of love, but a love which would *never* let me down, because it was not my love but God's love for me.

From love, my journey led me to loneliness. Through the fear of loneliness and the agony of its grip on me I could not see a solution. 'I have no control over it, but surely God does,' I thought to myself. God would help me to overcome my feelings of loneliness. My prayers were not answered.

Suddenly I realised that it was the *fear* of loneliness that I should be praying about, not loneliness itself, because there had to be a reason for my suffering. I turned to the Bible for an explanation. There in Isaiah I found this passage:

> Do not be afraid – I am with you!
> I am your God – let nothing terrify you!
> I will make you strong and help you:
> I will protect you and save you.

(Isaiah 41:10)

God did not take my loneliness from me, but He removed the fears and showed me that something very special would develop through these times. As it says in Paul's second letter to the Corinthians, 'For when I am weak, then I am strong' (2 Corinthians 12:10).

My fear of loneliness had gone, but I still held my fear of the uncertainty of the future. It took a long time for this to be released, because I could not grasp the fact that the future should be in God's hands and not mine. But my worries over what the future held, and the many failed plans, disappeared when I handed it all over to God. I read a passage in the Psalms which told me, 'The LORD says, "I will teach you the way you should go; I will instruct you and advise you'"(Psalm 32:8).

'Okay Lord,' I said, 'It's in Your hands; do what you will.'

I do not know if He took that as a challenge but He certainly had some dramatic, surprising and exciting happenings in store for me!

The hardest stage in my journey was overcoming past pain and not letting it affect the present or the future, and also, totally forgiving the people who had caused me anguish. I had to come face-to-face with events which had happened, to accept that I could not change the past but could grieve for what was missing in my life as a child and move into learning how to handle life now. I knew that I could not spend too long going over the past or the pain would increase and actually keep me a victim to agonising memories. Once I had been open and faced the hurts of the past, I had to choose to let go of them in order to be free: tell myself that what happened belonged then and not now. I saw that I had a choice: either I could hold on to the pain and let it destroy me or I could hand it over to God and let Him build something precious out of it. No, I would not forget events of the past, but equally I did not need to hold the happenings against the people who had hurt me.

I was particularly close to God during this part of my journey. He was very good to me, restoring my self-confidence, forgiving my sins, leading and upholding me, but there were times when He seemed distant and I could not reach Him. On one such occasion I went over to Greyfriars church to see Joan. Her understanding of the situation helped me enormously.

'You're on a bumpy road and God is the only one who can make it straight. You have to ask Him to guide you over the bumps and to enter into the worst places with you in order that the hills may gradually become flat.'

I realised where I had gone wrong: I was not putting *all* my trust in God. I thought of that wonderful verse in James: 'But when you pray, you must believe and not doubt at all. Whoever doubts is like a wave in the sea that is driven and blown about by the wind' (James 1:6).

Joan went on to talk about the importance of prayer in healing pain, and of putting everything before God's judgement and not our own. She read a passage from the Bible:

Trust in the Lord with all your heart. Never rely on what you think you know. Remember the LORD in everything you do, and he will show you the right way. Never let yourself think that you are wiser than you are; simply obey the LORD and refuse to do wrong. If you do, it will be like good medicine, healing your wounds and easing your pain (Proverbs 3:5-8).

I went home feeling reassured and with the knowledge that much prayer was needed. I brought all my troubles before God and asked that He would forgive my sins. A tranquillity filled my body and mind as I lay in the understanding that all around me was God, next to me was Jesus and inside me was the Holy Spirit. Yet there was no division between them; they were three in one. I asked God to show me a verse in the Bible. It read:

I have swept your sins away like a cloud.
Come back to me; I am the one who saves you.

(Isaiah 44:22)

21 | *YOUR WONDROUS LOVE PREVAILS*

*Though human nature
    fails,
Your wondrous love
    prevails,
To take darkness into
    light
And make us perfect in
    Your sight.*

*Redeemed by Your own
    Son,
God incarnate three in
    one,
You paid the price of
    life
With the burden of
    our strife.*

(Aged 19)

I awoke the next morning I had a strange sensation of having been re-created. I felt calm and filled with happiness. I felt differently towards God: I was far more aware of His presence, of my love for Him and my dependence on Him. I saw how hollow life had been before I came to know Him as Father; how I was created in His image and so without Him there would be a vacuum inside me. Even the world appeared to have changed: I saw a new beauty in nature, the delicate flowers, graceful trees, the brilliant rays of the sun and the dramatic formation of the sky. As I walked outside to hear the melodious singing of the birds, smell the sweet perfume of the multi-coloured blossom and see the wonderful array of greenery, I had a compulsive desire to express my feelings through poetry and art. This resulted in a burst of creativity.

While I was spending much of my time painting for pleasure it was decided that Greyfriars church needed a mural. It was for one of the rooms being converted into a meeting place and coffee bar for the unemployed, to be known as the Daybreak Centre. Members of Crossroads were asked to submit designs if they were interested. Claire's picture, simple and incorporating the word 'Daybreak', was chosen for the main wall, but as she had sent it in anonymously at the time I was asked to paint the mural.

One afternoon when I was balancing on the top of a ladder with paint dribbling down my arm, a man walked into the room who was to play an important part in the next stage of my life. As we talked, I discovered that He was the administrator of the new Greyfriars Centre, attached to the church, which houses a sports hall and various smaller rooms, including a book and craft shop and a coffee lounge. John and I started to discuss writing and art, and on hearing that I was writing *Puppet on a String*, a book about my experience with anorexia which had been accepted for publication, he suggested the possibility of a promotion day at the Centre. He also expressed interest in my own design for the Daybreak Centre and asked whether I had given any thought to getting it printed.

At a later stage, when John and I had been able to talk at greater length, all the possibilities seemed to come together. As I started to do more painting, he suggested that I use the Centre to exhibit and sell my work. This was a real incentive and inspiration and I found it exciting that so many good things were arising from the gift of my time in the painting of that mural.

Shortly after the mural had been completed I went with Crossroads for a camping weekend on a farm near Andover. I benefited a great deal from these few days, which held some very precious moments, and looking back I realise that there were two main reasons for my being there: to enable me to become more open and to gain a new insight into suffering.

We arrived on the Friday evening to find ourselves in the most beautifully peaceful surroundings. The girls' tents, sleeping about six people each, were pitched in the farmhouse garden. The boys' tents shared a field with the cows! Our meeting place was a large and exceptionally well-equipped barn. Besides a collection of straw bales to sit on, there was a long wooden table where the whole group could be seated for meals, several skittle alleys, a sink, and electrical points which were used for the kettle and electric piano. It was here that we met each morning and evening to sing, pray and listen to the talks.

It was an opportunity to get to know the other members of Crossroads far better. In the wonderfully relaxed atmosphere I really began to feel a part of the group and valued as one of its members. I became less introverted and my past feelings of not belonging completely disappeared.

The leaders exhausted us mentally, cramming a great many of the teachings of the Bible into a very short time, and also succeeded in exhausting us physically. Under the brilliant sun of what must have been one of England's hottest summers, we played rounders, cricket and football, among numerous other activities.

The talks given throughout the weekend were based on the letter of James in the New Testament. The letter begins by talking about suffering, and it was this section which had an incredible impact on me and left me deep in thought for the rest of the camp and many weeks after.

My brothers, consider yourselves fortunate when all kinds of trials come your way (James 1:2).

James was telling us to consider ourselves fortunate in times of trial, which seemed crazy until I realised the explanation which followed:

For you know that when your faith succeeds in facing such trials, the result is the ability to endure.

(James 1:3)

I saw that it is not the suffering itself we should consider fortunate to have, but the good which comes out of our ability to face the suffering. James then goes on to tell us:

Make sure that your endurance carries you all the way without failing, so that you may be perfect and complete, lacking nothing (James 1:4).

It appears that James is stressing the utmost importance of battling with our trials until the very end, for only then will we gain from our suffering.

My past attitude towards suffering had been one of fear and resentment: it felt unfair that I should suffer or that things should not work out as I wanted them to. Until this time I had not had any concept of how suffering can result in growth and that there are always two ways of looking at things: one, it is not fair, and two, what can I learn through this? I did not see God as someone sending suffering upon me, but as using the suffering I had gone through as a tool to help me to understand other people's pain, and have a deeper relationship with Him. I realised through a verse in the first book of Peter that not only can suffering be used to bring a richness of character but that, in order for it to be used for good, we must put our complete trust in God.

> So then, those who suffer because it is God's will for them, should by their good actions trust themselves completely to their Creator, who always keeps his promise (1 Peter 4:19).

Peter also looked at suffering in the most wonderful way as a privilege.

> My dear friends, do not be surprised at the painful test you are suffering, as though something unusual were happening to you. Rather be glad that you are sharing Christ's sufferings, so that you may be full of joy when his glory is revealed (1 Peter 4:12-13).

When I read Paul's letter to the Romans at a later date he also seemed to speak of suffering as a privilege.

> Since we are his children, we all possess the blessings he keeps for his people, and we will also possess with Christ what God has kept for him; for if we share Christ's suffering, we will also share his glory. I consider that what we suffer at this present time cannot be compared at all with the glory that is going to be revealed to us (Romans 8:17-18).

This concept became more and more amazing to me, and I found myself actually thanking God for all that had happened over the years because I began to see the marvellous way in which He was beginning to use it. This, along with a verse I later found in the first book of Peter, gave me the strength to face times of trial and gain from them.

> God will bless you for this, if you endure the pain of undeserved suffering because you are conscious of his will (1 Peter 2:19).

I returned home with the knowledge that a new life lay ahead of me. I began to focus on the future and what I could make of it. Along with this came the need to become more independent: I took the opportunity to move out of my parents' home to my own bedsit near to the centre of Reading, so that I could be more a part of the church and learn to relate to the people I was getting to know both in the church and in the young people's group.

Although much joy and hope were coming into my life, I was well aware that life is not a bed of roses. I realised that I did not have to feel happy all the time in order to be fully recovered from anorexia. Up until this time I had thought that if I was feeling low or frustrated then it meant there was something wrong with me or I was slipping back. I began to see that life has its ups and downs and that, as people, we *feel* emotions. I learned that in life there may be times when we all have to *battle* with difficult circumstances, but it is how we cope with these difficult times that is important. Through the process of recovery I had learned how to cope through talking about and expressing my feelings to a few trusted friends. I no longer needed to cope by starving myself or having to achieve a certain weight. I no longer needed to have an anorexic identity, because I had an identity as a child of God and as a unique individual. I could be *me* and I knew who *me* was, because I knew the One who had created me. So much had changed inside me, in my thinking and in my feelings, that I could truly say goodbye to being anorexic. I realised that, to begin with, sustaining my freedom from anorexia would be a fight, but I also knew from God's promises that He would enable me to endure. I clung on to the words in Paul's first letter to the Corinthians:

But God keeps his promise, and he will not allow you to be tested beyond your power to remain firm; at the time you are put to the test, he will give you the strength to endure it, and so provide you with a way out.

(1 Corinthians 10:13)

I saw, through a verse which Joan gave me, that it is not only strength God gives us but inner tranquillity as we know His love.

> The Lord your God is with you,
> he is mighty to save.
> He will take great delight in you,
> he will quiet you with His love,
> he will rejoice over you with singing.
>
> (Zephaniah 3:17 NIV)

With all these things behind me, at 19, I find great beauty and comfort in the following words from Isaiah:

> But the Lord says,
> 'Do not cling to events of the past
> or dwell on what happened long ago.
> Watch for the new thing I am going to do.
> It is happening already – you can see
> it now!
> I will make a road through the wilderness
> and give you streams of water there'.
>
> (Isaiah 43:18-19)

LOOKING BACK

Looking back I can hardly believe that the words I wrote in *Puppet on a String* are about me! Yet in re-reading the book, making some alterations and finding more of my poems to add for this edition of *Puppet on a String*, I felt the heartache, frustration and pain I experienced all those years ago. I can also see so clearly how God had His hand upon my life, directing me to certain people at certain times, all of whom played such important roles in my recovery. Not long ago I was taking a day seminar on understanding eating disorders and one of the organisers was someone who had faithfully prayed for me throughout my fight to beat anorexia. She had not seen me since those days! It seemed so strange to meet her as an adult and as someone on the same wavelength, when my memories were of me as a fearful and distant teenager and her as an older woman who was a part of what I thought was a 'fuddy-duddy' group who prayed for me! At the time I felt awkward and did not think their prayers would do anything. Here I was, standing before her as evidence that God heard and God healed. Now that I am in the position of praying for others, and probably praying quite similar prayers, I am so full of appreciation and admiration for her commitment to me. There are so many other people I could speak of in the same light: people who maybe I did not really appreciate in the past but who I now know played a significant part in the sequence of events which led to my recovery.

You may be wondering what happened to some of the people in *Puppet on a String*. Their outcome brings both joy and pain. Perhaps most painful was the untimely, tragic and cruel death of my cousin Kathie whilst the first edition of *Puppet on a String* was at the publishers. The book was dedicated to Kathie as someone who meant so much to me as a desperately unhappy teenager. For years I found it impossible to sing the hymn 'When I survey the wondrous cross' which Kathie sang as a solo in Bermuda Cathedral and which I chose for her funeral. But time has brought great healing.

The little Salvation Army man who visited me in hospital and sent me flowers on my return home went to be with the Lord, but not before He had attended the launch of *Puppet on a String*, during which time his bright eyes twinkled as he too witnessed a walking miracle to his prayers. My boyfriend Andy asked me to marry him, also around the time that the first edition of *Puppet on a String* was published, but months later the engagement broke off. The girls at the CYFA camp I never saw again, with the exception of my school friend Mary who has remained in contact with me. Frances, who rescued me that fateful day the Headmistress sent me to the city to apologise to the nuns is still in touch. I am godmother to two of her four boys! Tania did become a doctor, as had been her desire since the age of five, and we meet whenever we can; even if months or years have gone by, as soon as we start to talk it is as though we saw each other only yesterday! She married and has very recently become a mum to a little girl. My parents have retired and are very supportive of the work I do, and my sister Ruth is engrossed in horses, her passion from childhood. We are no longer 'enemies,' but we remain very different from each other.

There are many people I could update you on, but this in itself would be another book. The first edition of *Puppet on a String* ended literally at the point of me choosing to say goodbye to anorexia. As those who have recovered from anorexia know, only the test of time proves whether recovery lasts. It was a vulnerable point at which to end a book, although I am glad that at the time I did not know the extent of the vulnerability. I had declared myself recovered, and there was no time to prove that it was going to be long-lasting. Not only was there no time, but I was thrown into a world of extreme pressure with the media putting me on a pedestal as one of the first people to write about my experience and prove that anorexia could be overcome completely, and with anorexics everywhere desperate to talk to me.

The years which followed after I wrote *Puppet on a String* were years of growth, learning and strengthening of a genuine decision I had already made: that I would not go back into the anorexic way again. Each year brought a greater degree of freedom, not just in respect of eating but in confidence and communication, for recovery is not merely about overcoming a battle with eating, it is about maturity and flexibility in life. My life today, as someone who has recovered from anorexia, is quite different from how my life was when I first recovered, because I have grown as a person as well as having learned how to change the anorexic ways of eating, thinking and relating. Anorexia is not only to do with food, it is a whole way of conducting your life: you are anorexic in your communication with people and the way you live as well as in the relationship you have with food. Freedom means freedom from all aspects of anorexia, not only eating and weight-related issues.

You might also be wondering whether I have had any long-term effects through the years I abused my body with the anorexia. For several years afterwards I suffered terrible pain in my bones, which I believe was as a result of vitamin and mineral deficiencies. For a long period I suffered from an allergy to some foods along with a weakening of my immune system and symptoms similar to M.E. None of these actually affected my eating patterns, and with nutritional advice and prayer the allergies went and I became strong and healthy. I reached, and have since happily maintained, a steady weight of around 9 stone. Food is an enjoyable part of my life and I love it!

Today I know that I am left with no long-term side effects from the anorexia, and I thank God for this. I have yet to find out whether I can have children, but then I am also waiting for a husband too! This in itself will be the makings of another book! When I was 14 my grandfather said that I would be a writer and writing is one of my greatest joys (except when working to a deadline). Perhaps I will write another update in another 20 years, by which time I will be 60 – now *that* I do find hard to believe! Maybe I will stick to writing a novel set in the African bush!

Nicholaston House
Christian Healing Centre

The vision for Nicholaston House came about long before it was purchased. Some 13 years prior to the House coming on the market in 1998, a group of Christians in a Methodist Chapel, in a rural location on Gower, began praying for a place where people could get away from the stresses of life to receive help and rest. They believed that God would bring the Centre into being and that their role was to pray for it. Meanwhile a couple in Surrey received a vision for 'a place where people who are hurting could come and find space'. A series of God-ordained events resulted in that couple, Derrick and Sue Hancock, moving to Swansea, becoming involved in Swansea City Mission, and the Mission purchasing Nicholaston House. Other people who now work at Nicholaston House also had similar visions for a residential centre for healing, and hence the House is born out of the prayers, visions and longings of several people who, over the years, have had a heart to see God bring healing and restoration to broken lives.

In the entrance of the House are the words, 'In this place I will give peace'. People frequently comment on the peace they experience during their stay and the ways in which they encounter the presence of God in the House. As well as coming for rest, space and ministry, people come to Nicholaston House to participate in the week and weekend courses and retreats on offer. These events include prayer ministry, time out, creative activities, spiritual encouragement, and insight and support for those addressing a number of personal issues, such as eating disorders.

The location of the House itself is ideal for rest and renewal. Set in the heart of the Gower Peninsula, an area of outstanding natural beauty, Nicholaston House overlooks the stunning Bay of Oxwich with its vast expanse of sand. In contrast, a country lane separates the back of the House from Cefn Bryn, where sheep, ponies and cattle roam free across miles of open moorland. The whole area creates an ambiance of peace and tranquillity.

Inside the House, the downstairs comprises a sea-facing dining room, conservatory and lounge, a craft and bookstall and two medium-sized conference rooms. The conference rooms can be opened up into one large room seating over 100 people.

Upstairs there is a lounge and a small chapel and library, as well as accommodation for around 28 people. All the bedrooms are en-suite (most are twin) and have colour television and tea and coffee making facilities. Many are sea-facing, and a passenger lift, as well as the main staircase, serve all. One bedroom is specifically adapted for those with disabilities – including wheelchair users. The disabled toilets, ramps and lift, make the House available to all.

The gardens, which overlook the sea, are designed to encourage relaxation and the House is a member of the Quiet Gardens Trust.

In order to find out more about the work of Nicholaston House, you can visit the website or write and ask for an information pack (which includes details of the work, in-house events and resources). If you would like your name added to the mailing list, which means you will be kept up-to-date with latest news on events and will receive a bi-annual newsletter, please send a large SAE to:

Nicholaston House, Penmaen, Gower, Swansea SA3 2HL
Tel: 01792 371317 Fax: 01792 371217
Email: managers@nicholastonhouse.org
Website: www.nicholastonhouse.org